Company's Coming

Kids Do SNACKS

Fun food for kids to make Jean Paré

visit our website at **www.companyscoming.com**

Front Cover

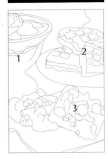

1 Yum-Yum Yogurt Layers, page 27
2 Ham & Cheese Wafflewich, page 53
3 Hokey Pokey Squares, page 120

Kids Do Snacks
Copyright © Company's Coming Publishing Limited

First Printing July 2007

Library and Archives Canada Cataloguing in Publication
Paré, Jean, date
Kids do snacks / Jean Paré.
(Original series)
Includes index.
ISBN 978-1-897069-27-1
1. Cookery—Juvenile literature. I. Title. II. Series.
TX652.5.P385 2007   j641.5'123   C2007-900111-4

Published by
Company's Coming Publishing Limited
2311 – 96 Street
Edmonton, Alberta, Canada T6N 1G3
Tel: 780-450-6223 Fax: 780-450-1857
www.companyscoming.com

We acknowledge the financial support of the Government of Canada
through the Book Publishing Industry Development Program (BPIDP)
for our publishing activities.

Printed in Canada

Editor: Amy Hough

*We gratefully acknowledge the following
suppliers for their generous support of
our Test and Photography Kitchens:*

Broil King Barbecues
Corelle®
Hamilton Beach® Canada
Lagostina®
Proctor Silex® Canada
Tupperware®

*Our special thanks to the following
businesses for providing props for
photography:*

Casa Bugatti
Cherison Enterprises Inc.
Chintz & Company
Danesco Inc.
Le Gnome
Linens N' Things
Mikasa Home Store
Out of the Fire Studio
Pyrex®
Stokes
The Bay
The Dazzling Gourmet
Wiltshire®
Winners Stores

Table of Contents

Cookbot 3000

Creampuff

Monsieur Auk-Auk

Attention Adults!

Those of you who know our books, know we love to cook—and we love to get others hooked on cooking, too! And kids are no exception.
The confidence children can get from preparing their own food is quite inspiring—and if they can share it with an adult or a friend? Talk about a sense of accomplishment!

We're often surprised at how cookbooks for kids don't actually have recipes kids can make themselves—it really doesn't make sense. Often they feature recipes kids would like but a willing adult is expected to make. Or they feature recipes that allow the kid to stir or do some decorating while the adult does the rest of the work. That may be fine for very little kids but how about the kids who are ready to actually start cooking on their own? Well this book is designed for them. Each recipe is written in a way they will understand. We feel confident that kids can actually make these recipes themselves. This is a cookbook for kids, after all!

This doesn't exclude the adult of the house from participating, though.
We recommend that an adult always look over the recipe that is going to be prepared, and make sure it is suitable for the skill level of the young chef-in-training. We also suggest that an adult be on hand to supervise, in case any questions or concerns arise (think of this as an excellent *fun* learning opportunity).

Now, a little about how this book is structured: Company's Coming believes children need to feel good about themselves when they do something well, so we've created recipes that work for kids with various cooking skills.
As the chapters progress throughout the book, the skills required to complete the recipes increase. This means kids who are just starting in the kitchen should begin with the first chapter and work their way through the book as they start to acquire more and more confidence in the kitchen. And for kids who already know how to work with all the various cooking methods, they'll be able to make anything from any of the chapters. We believe structuring the book this way serves 2 purposes: it allows the adult to guide the kids to chapters that are suitable for their skill levels; and it allows kids to work on the many different techniques and methods involved in cooking.

Not only will kids gain confidence and skills from using *Kids Do Snacks*, but there's also an added bonus—they might just need you to sample their wares!

Jean Paré

Nutrition Information Guidelines

Each recipe is analyzed using the most current version of the Canadian Nutrient File from Health Canada, which is based on the United States Department of Agriculture (USDA) Nutrient Database.

- If more than one ingredient is listed (such as "butter or hard margarine"), or if a range is given (1 – 2 tsp., 5 – 10 mL), only the first ingredient or first amount is analyzed.

- For meat, poultry and fish, the serving size per person is based on the recommended 4 oz. (113 g) uncooked weight (without bone), which is 2 – 3 oz. (57 – 85 g) cooked weight (without bone)— approximately the size of a deck of playing cards.

- Milk used is 2% M.F. (milk fat), unless otherwise stated.

- Cooking oil used is canola oil, unless otherwise stated.

- Ingredients indicating "sprinkle," "optional," or "for garnish" are not included in the nutrition information.

- The fat in recipes and combination foods can vary greatly depending on the sources and types of fats used in each specific ingredient. For these reasons, the amount of saturated, monounsaturated and polyunsaturated fats may not add up to the total fat content.

Vera C. Mazurak, Ph.D.
Nutritionist

Monsieur Auk-Auk

Although born and raised in the freezing climate of Antarctica, Monsieur Auk-Auk could never quite get used to the cold. It was his dislike of all things icy that led him to his love of cooking. One day while munching on his usual diet of frozen krill-sicles, he had a brainstorm. *"Mon Dieu!"* He exclaimed, *"Mon* krill would be so much better if it was not so *froid*—and was covered in a tasty sauce, *non*?"

It was this revelation that inspired Monsieur Auk-Auk to leave Antarctica and journey north. During his travels, he learned to make emu omelettes in Australia, jambalaya in Louisiana and poutine in Quebec, where he now resides and stars in the French-Canadian cooking show *Savoureux Num-Nums*.

Creampuff

Born in the fiery depths of the Hawaiian volcano Kilauea, Creampuff lived a solitary life trying to evade the peeping eyes of tourists. Because most of the earth's people don't believe in dragons, and proving the existence of one could make a person quite rich, Creampuff was forced to hide himself away from the world so he wouldn't be put in a zoo or a research facility.

It was not until Creampuff got his Internet connection that he developed his love of cooking. If there's a recipe on the Internet, he's tried it! By posting such recipes as Flambéed Fire Dim Sum and Lava-Alarm Chili, he gained the reputation of being one of the best Internet chefs around. As an added bonus he's become less lonely—through the Internet he's made many friends with other, very real, mythological creatures. Amongst his best friends he counts the Abominable Snowman, Ogopogo and Leprechaun Lou.

Cookbot 3000

Cookbot 3000 began life under very strange circumstances. Created by failed chef Roc Hardbiskut, Cookbot was originally designed to wreak havoc in the kitchens of rival chefs. The plan was simple: Cookbot would apply for jobs in the best kitchens throughout the world, and as soon as he was hired he would begin stealing the rival chefs' cooking secrets and recipes. And when people would visit the restaurant, he would serve them horribly smelly food.

That was the plan—but Cookbot failed miserably. There was something in him—perhaps a crossed wire or a microchip glitch—that wouldn't allow him to ruin any meal. He just couldn't do it. Chef Hardbiskut was enraged and threw Cookbot out his apartment window. Dented, but happy to be free of Chef Hardbiskut, Cookbot has since made it his life's work to travel the streets of the world cooking food for anyone who is hungry and has 25 cents (which he donates to the Home for Disgruntled and Misunderstood Robots).

Keeping Everything Cool in the Kitchen

With great snack making comes great responsibility. To avoid being a complete spaz in the kitchen, pay attention to the following points:

Before you begin basics:

- Make sure an adult is OK with you cooking and using the ingredients you need.
- If you have long hair, tie it up and out of the way.
- Roll up long sleeves and tuck in baggy shirts.
- Read the recipe all the way through.
- Wash your hands.
- Get your ingredients washed and ready.
- Gather the proper equipment in the sizes recommended in the recipe.

While you're cooking basics:

- Do one recipe step at a time. The numbers beside our ingredients match the steps to keep you on track. Don't skip steps.
- Make sure to use oven mitts when handling hot pots and pans.
- When using the stove, always turn handles inward so you don't knock off any pots and pans.

After your masterpiece snack has been made basics:

- Turn off the stove or oven.
- Clean up—or no one will ever let you cook again!

Kids Do Snacks

Top Chef Tools

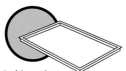

Baking Sheet
Looks like a cookie sheet but it has sides—so things won't roll on to the floor!

Dry Measures
Use these to measure dry ingredients. To measure dry stuff properly, spoon it into your cup, and then level off any extra with the straight side of a table knife.

Grater
Perfect for grating carrots or cheese. Go slowly so you don't accidentally grate your fingers!

Ladle
Great for spooning out soups.

Liquid Measures
You guessed it—these measure liquids. Pour in your liquid and set on an even surface. Check at eye level to see if the liquid reaches the mark.

Measuring Spoons
Make sure ingredients are levelled off, unless the recipe calls for a "heaping" spoonful.

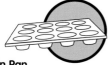

Muffin Pan
Good for making muffins or holding Dixie cups in place when you have to fill a lot of them. Mini-muffin pans look sort-of the same—except the cups are mini-sized.

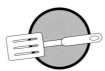

Pancake Lifter
Slides under pancakes without tearing them.

Pastry brush
Use this to put liquid on pastry.

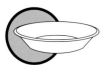

Pie plate
A circular tin for baking.

Ramekins
Little cups that can be put in the oven.

Rolling pin
Great for getting pastry flat.

Saucepan
Sometimes called a pot. Always use the size called for in the recipe.

Serrated knife
Great for cutting softer things like bread.

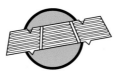

Strainer
An easy way to drain liquid—always use it over a sink.

Oven with Rack Positions
It's important to follow the recipe instructions for rack positions.

Whisk
A tool that mixes ingredients really well and breaks up lumps.

Wire Rack
Good for cooling baked items by letting air flow underneath.

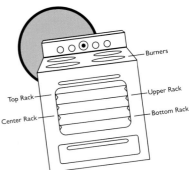

Burners

Top Rack

Center Rack

Upper Rack

Bottom Rack

Blend It!

If you're new to cooking, or you just love to turn solid things into liquid, this is the section for you. In *Blend It!* you don't need a knife for cutting, you just need to know how to measure and, of course, work your blender.

find 20 vegetables

```
G X Z Q M N C O R N Z R E
R R M O O R H S U M E J C
E Z E I C L O E G W Q A U
E T N E E G K O V S S T
N O U E N A L L R P X Q T
B M K I B O F E A A G U E
E U K B L I N R R Z P A L
A E A H L O A I K Y I S B
N C T U X G C E O X N H E
A Z A N U G D C J N R K E
S C P S C A R R O T U P T
O T A T O P A E P R T Z M
B E A N S P R O U T B F M
```

ASPARAGUS	BEANSPROUT	BEET
BROCCOLI	CABBAGE	CARROT
CAULIFLOWER	CELERY	CORN
GREENBEAN	GREENONION	LEEK
LETTUCE	MUSHROOM	OKRA
ONION	PEA	POTATO
SQUASH	TURNIP	

Berry Me Alive, below

Berry Me Alive

Sound scary? It is! If you don't drink it quick, it will get so thick you'll have to dig yourself out with a spoon!

Get It Together: liquid measures, measuring spoons, dry measures, blender, 2 glasses

1.			
Milk	1 1/4 cups	300 mL
Frozen mixed berries	1 cup	250 mL
Raspberry yogurt	1 cup	250 mL
Orange juice	1/3 cup	75 mL
Instant vanilla pudding powder	2 tbsp.	30 mL

1. Put all 5 ingredients into blender. Cover with lid. Blend until smooth. Pour into glasses. Makes about 3 1/2 cups (875 mL)—enough for 2 kids.

1 serving: 279 Calories; 4.5 g Total Fat (trace Mono, trace Poly, 2.9 g Sat); 20 mg Cholesterol; 49 g Carbohydrate; 3 g Fibre; 11 g Protein; 358 mg Sodium

Pictured above.

Man-Go-Go Smoothie

Grab some mango when it's time to go-go and you'll have all the energy you need!

Get It Together: liquid measures, dry measures, blender, tall glass

1.	Frozen chopped mango	1 cup	250 mL
	Apple juice	3/4 cup	175 mL
	Vanilla frozen yogurt	1/2 cup	125 mL

1. Put all 3 ingredients into blender. Cover with lid. Blend until smooth. Pour into glass. Makes about 1 3/4 cups (425 mL)—enough for 1 thirsty kid.

1 serving: 330 Calories; 5.0 g Total Fat (0.2 g Mono, 0.1 g Poly, 3.1 g Sat); 15 mg Cholesterol; 71 g Carbohydrate; 3 g Fibre; 4 g Protein; 56 mg Sodium

Pictured on page 11.

Milky Way Blue Lemonade

Pucker up, kiddo! When life gives you blueberries, make lemonade milk!

Get It Together: dry measures, liquid measures, measuring spoons, blender, glass

1.	Frozen blueberries	1/2 cup	125 mL
	Milk	1/3 cup	75 mL
	Frozen concentrated lemonade	3 tbsp.	50 mL
	Ice cubes	3	3

1. Put all 4 ingredients into blender. Cover with lid. Blend until smooth. Pour into glass. Makes about 1 1/4 cups (300 mL)—a refreshing drink, just for you.

1 serving: 178 Calories; 2.3 g Total Fat (0 g Mono, trace Poly, 1.0 g Sat); 7 mg Cholesterol; 39 g Carbohydrate; 2 g Fibre; 3 g Protein; 44 mg Sodium

Pictured on page 11.

Q: When do you stop at green and go at red?

A: When you're eating a watermelon.

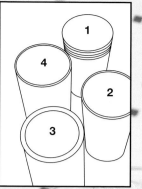

Marshmallow Fruit Soda Pop

Ever try drinking a marshmallow? Here's your chance! Use other frozen fruit if you like.

Get It Together: dry measures, liquid measures, blender, 2 large glasses, spoon

1. **Frozen strawberries**	2 1/2 cups	625 mL
Orange juice	1 cup	250 mL
2. **Jar of marshmallow creme**	7 oz.	198 g
3. **Club soda**	1 cup	250 mL

1. Put strawberries and orange juice into blender. Cover with lid. Blend until almost smooth. There should still be some tiny chunks of strawberry.
2. Add marshmallow creme. Blend until mixed. Pour into glasses.
3. Add 1/2 cup (125 mL) club soda to each glass. Stir. Makes about 3 1/3 cups (835 mL)—enough for you and a friend.

1 serving: 442 Calories; 0 g Total Fat (0 g Mono, 0 g Poly, 0 g Sat); 0 mg Cholesterol; 110 g Carbohydrate; 4 g Fibre; 2 g Protein; 90 mg Sodium

Pictured on page 11.

Fruit Sludgies

Everybody likes to drink sludge, don't they? Not sure? Give it a go and you'll be a sludge eater in no time!

Get It Together: can opener, dry measures, ice cream scoop, liquid measures, blender, 2 glasses

1. **Can of fruit cocktail, drained**	14 oz.	398 mL
Lime sherbet	2/3 cup	150 mL
Milk	1/2 cup	125 mL

1. Put all 3 ingredients into blender. Cover with lid. Blend until almost smooth. Pour into glasses. Makes about 2 1/4 cups (550 mL)—enough for 2 sludge eaters.

1 serving: 239 Calories; 2.4 g Total Fat (0.3 g Mono, 0.1 g Poly, 0.4 g Sat); 8 mg Cholesterol; 56 g Carbohydrate; 3 g Fibre; 3 g Protein; 66 mg Sodium

Pictured on page 11.

(continued on next page)

Blend It!

Cookbot 3000 Tip: Use a different flavour of sherbet to change the flavour and colour of your sludgie! Or make it into a slushie by adding 2 or 3 ice cubes with the other ingredients before blending.

Chocolate Galaxies

This chocolate and vanilla-swirled treat is out of this world—
and ready in less than 10 minutes!

Get It Together: liquid measures, dry measures, blender, 2 dessert dishes, measuring spoons, table knife

1. **Milk**	**1 cup**	**250 mL**
Instant chocolate pudding powder	**1/3 cup**	**75 mL**
(half of 4-serving size box)		
2. **Vanilla yogurt**	**1/4 cup**	**60 mL**

1. Put milk into blender. Add pudding powder. Cover with lid. Blend until smooth. Pour pudding mixture into dessert dishes.

2. Spoon 2 tbsp. (30 mL) yogurt on top of each bowl of pudding. Stir pudding and yogurt together with tip of knife to make spirals. Wait for about 5 minutes until thickened. Makes about 2 1/3 cups (575 mL)—enough for you and a friend.

1 serving: 214 Calories; 3.4 g Total Fat (0.9 g Mono, 0.2 g Poly, 1.9 g Sat); 11 mg Cholesterol; 41 g Carbohydrate; 1 g Fibre; 6 g Protein; 628 mg Sodium

Pictured below.

Chocolate Galaxies, above

Butterscotch Me Up Dip

Give fruit, graham crackers, cookies or even raisin toast a dunk in this sweet dip.

Get It Together: liquid measures, dry measures, blender, spoon, small bowl

1.	**Milk**	**1/2 cup**	**125 mL**
	Vanilla yogurt	**1/2 cup**	**125 mL**
	Instant butterscotch pudding powder	**1/3 cup**	**75 mL**
	(half of 4-serving size box)		

1. Put all 3 ingredients into blender. Cover with lid. Blend until mixture is smooth and thickened. Spoon into bowl. Makes about 1 1/4 cups (300 mL)—enough for you and a friend to go dip crazy.

1 serving: 168 Calories; 2.0 g Total Fat (0 g Mono, 0 g Poly, 1.3 g Sat); 9 mg Cholesterol; 31 g Carbohydrate; 1 g Fibre; 6 g Protein; 201 mg Sodium

Pictured on page 15.

Cookbot 3000 Tip: Mix it up a bit and try other pudding flavours. Make a healthier snack by using sugar-free pudding and low-fat yogurt.

I'm A Little Nutty Dip

Go nuts for this smooth dip that's great with fruit, veggies and crackers.

Get It Together: liquid measures, dry measures, blender, small bowl, spoon

1.	**Vanilla yogurt**	**1 cup**	**250 mL**
	Peanut butter	**1/3 cup**	**75 mL**

1. Put yogurt and peanut butter into blender. Cover with lid. Blend until smooth. Spoon into bowl. Makes about 1 1/3 cups (325 mL)—enough dip for 2 nutty kids.

1 serving: 325 Calories; 23.4 g Total Fat (10.4 g Mono, 5.9 g Poly, 5.4 g Sat); 8 mg Cholesterol; 16 g Carbohydrate; 2 g Fibre; 16 g Protein; 87 mg Sodium

Pictured on page 15.

Confusing Dip

Is it sweet or is it sour? This confusing dip is both but, thankfully, it's delicious, too! Munch with veggies.

Cookbot 3000 Tip: To soften cream cheese, let it sit on the counter for about 30 minutes.

Get It Together: liquid measures, measuring spoons, dry measures, blender, spoon, small bowl

1.			
	Apricot jam	1/2 cup	125 mL
	Cream cheese, softened	4 oz.	125 g
	Apple cider vinegar	2 tbsp.	30 mL
	Soy sauce	2 tbsp.	30 mL
	Hoisin sauce	1 tsp.	5 mL

1. Put all 5 ingredients into blender. Cover with lid. Blend until smooth. Spoon into bowl. Makes about 1 1/3 cups (325 mL)—enough for 2 confused kids.

1 serving: 411 Calories; 20.3 g Total Fat (0.1 g Mono, 0.1 g Poly, 14.0 g Sat); 60 mg Cholesterol; 57 g Carbohydrate; trace Fibre; 6 g Protein; 1065 mg Sodium

Pictured on page 15.

4 O'Clock Fiesta Salsa

It's a fine time for a pre-dinner fiesta. This beany salsa is great on tortilla chips, crackers or even toast!

Get It Together: can opener, dry measures, liquid measures, measuring spoons, food processor, spoon, small dish

1.			
	Canned white kidney beans, rinsed and drained	1 cup	250 mL
	Salsa	1/4 cup	60 mL
	Spreadable cream cheese	1/4 cup	60 mL
	Lime juice	1 tbsp.	15 mL

1. Put all 4 ingredients into food processor. Cover with lid. Process until almost smooth. If necessary, stop food processor and scrape down sides. Spoon into dish. Makes about 1 1/3 cups (325 mL)—enough for you and a friend.

1 serving: 217 Calories; 11.0 g Total Fat (0 g Mono, 0 g Poly, 7.0 g Sat); 30 mg Cholesterol; 21 g Carbohydrate; 6 g Fibre; 8 g Protein; 381 mg Sodium

Pictured on page 15.

Cookbot 3000 Tip: The remaining beans can be frozen for another time or added to a soup, salad or stew.

Mix It!

We've mixed it up in this chapter. You'll need to do cutting for some of the recipes—but not all of them. You'll also need to know how to grate.

Q1: What do corn wear to bed?

Q2: What do you take before every meal?

Q3: Why did the chicken cross the playground?

Answers: Q1: Silk Q2: A seat Q3: To get to the other slide

Swimming Fruit Sipper

It's fruit overboard in this ginger ale and fruit drink!

Get It Together: liquid measures, sharp knife, cutting board, tall glass, mixing spoon

1.	Ginger ale	1/2 cup	125 mL
	White grape (or white cranberry) juice	1/2 cup	125 mL
2.	Fresh strawberries, quartered	2	2
	Seedless green grapes, halved	6	6
	Canned mandarin orange segments, halved	8	8

1. Pour ginger ale and juice into glass. Mix gently.

2. Carefully drop in 4 strawberry pieces, 6 grape halves and 8 halved orange segments. Repeat with remaining fruit. Makes about 1 1/2 cups (375 mL)—enough for 1 kid.

1 serving: *174 Calories; 0.2 g Total Fat (0 g Mono, trace Poly, 0.1 g Sat); 0 mg Cholesterol; 43 g Carbohydrate; 1 g Fibre; 1 g Protein; 17 mg Sodium*

Pictured on page 19.

 Creampuff Tip: Use any combination of your favourite fruit. Watermelon, pineapple, apple, pear, kiwi, honeydew or cantaloupe, they all work!

Apple Of My Iced Tea

Time for a tea party! Wow a friend with this extreme iced tea that has an amazing apple taste!

Get It Together: liquid measures, measuring spoons, pitcher, mixing spoon, 2 large glasses

1.	Apple juice	1 cup	250 mL
	Cold water	3/4 cup	175 mL
	Lemon iced tea crystals	2 tbsp.	30 mL
2.	Ice cubes		

1. Pour apple juice and water into pitcher. Add crystals. Stir until crystals are dissolved. Pour into glasses.

(continued on next page)

2. Add ice cubes. Makes about 2 cups (500 mL)—enough for you and the apple of your eye.

1 serving: 95 Calories; 0 g Total Fat (0 g Mono, 0 g Poly, 0 g Sat); 0 mg Cholesterol; 24 g Carbohydrate; 0 g Fibre; 0 g Protein; 5 mg Sodium

Pictured below.

Creampuff Tip: Experiment with other juices like cranberry peach.

Left: Swimming Fruit Sipper, page 18 Right: Apple Of My Iced Tea, page 18

Left: Curry Fury Dip, below   Right: Cheese Puck, page 21

Curry Fury Dip

Are you mad about curry? This dip will satisfy your curry craving in no time!
Eat with your favourite deli meats—just roll them up and dip. Or try with fruit
or veggie sticks.

Get It Together: measuring spoons, small bowl, whisk

1. | | | |
   |---|---|---|
   | Mayonnaise | 2 tbsp. | 30 mL |
   | Prepared mustard | 2 tbsp. | 30 mL |
   | Syrup | 4 tsp. | 20 mL |
   | Curry powder | 1/2 tsp. | 2 mL |
   | Salt, sprinkle | | |

1. Put all 5 ingredients into bowl. Stir with whisk until smooth.
   Makes about 1/3 cup (75 mL)—enough for 1 kid.

1 serving: 238 Calories; 15.5 g Total Fat (8.7 g Mono, 5.0 g Poly, 1.1 g Sat); 8 mg Cholesterol;
25 g Carbohydrate; 1 g Fibre; 2 g Protein; 523 mg Sodium

Pictured above.

Creampuff Tip: This dip can be served immediately or
covered with plastic wrap and chilled for you to eat later on.

Mix It!

Cheese Puck

Score off the ice with this spicy cheese puck. Spread on crackers, pita chips or tortilla chips.

Get It Together: dry measures, measuring spoons, grater, sharp knife, cutting board, small bowl, fork, mixing spoon, plate

1. Cream cheese, softened	1/4 cup	60 mL
Grated medium Cheddar cheese	2 tbsp.	30 mL
Grated Monterey Jack cheese	2 tbsp.	30 mL
Cajun seasoning	1/2 tsp.	2 mL
2. Finely chopped ham	3 tbsp.	50 mL
Crushed pecans	2 tbsp.	30 mL

1. Put cream cheese into bowl. Mash with fork until smooth. Add next 3 ingredients. Mix well.

2. Add ham and pecans. Mix well. Shape into a flattened ball using your hands. Place on plate. Makes enough for 2 hungry sports fans.

1 serving: 231 Calories; 20.8 g Total Fat (4.2 g Mono, 1.8 g Poly, 10.6 g Sat); 56 mg Cholesterol; 2 g Carbohydrate; 1 g Fibre; 10 g Protein; 334 mg Sodium

Pictured on page 20.

Creampuff Tip: To soften cream cheese, let it sit on the counter for about 30 minutes.

To crush pecans, place nuts in a resealable sandwich bag and roll a rolling pin over top until the nuts are crushed.

Q: What starts with t, ends with t and is filled with t?

A: A teapot.

4 Dipping Adventure

With 4 layers, this dip is 4 times the fun! Eat with veggies, tortilla chips or Micro-Chips, page 44.

Get It Together: measuring spoons, sharp knife, cutting board, grater, small bowl, fork, spoon, plate

1.	Spreadable cream cheese	3 tbsp.	50 mL
	Sour cream	2 tbsp.	30 mL
	Pepper, sprinkle		
2.	Salsa	2 tbsp.	30 mL
3.	Chopped green pepper	2 tbsp.	30 mL
	Chopped fresh tomato	1 tbsp.	15 mL
4.	Grated mozzarella cheese	2 tbsp.	30 mL

1. Put first 3 ingredients into bowl. Mix with fork until smooth. Spoon onto centre of plate. Spread cheese mixture into a 4 inch (10 cm) wide circle.
2. Spoon salsa over cream cheese mixture.
3. Sprinkle green pepper and tomato over salsa.
4. Sprinkle cheese on top. Makes enough for 2 adventurous kids.

1 serving: 130 Calories; 11.7 g Total Fat (1.2 g Mono, 0.2 g Poly, 7.8 g Sat); 34 mg Cholesterol; 3 g Carbohydrate; trace Fibre; 4 g Protein; 180 mg Sodium

Pictured on page 23.

Creampuff Tip: To make it spicier, add 1 chopped hot pepper ring to the cream cheese mixture. You could also use a spicier salsa or a grated jalapeño cheese blend instead of the mozzarella cheese.

Q: What did the grape say when he was sat on?

A: Nothing—he just let out a little whine.

Top: Rice Cream Cones, page 24
Bottom: 4 X 4 Dipping Adventure, page 22

Rice Cream Cones

Don't worry about this cone melting all over—it's filled with rice and veggies. What a neat treat!

Get It Together: measuring spoons, liquid measures, dry measures, sharp knife, cutting board, grater, vegetable peeler, medium bowl, mixing spoon, ice cream scoop

1.	Mayonnaise	1/4 cup	60 mL
	Apple cider vinegar	1 tsp.	5 mL
	Granulated sugar	1 tsp.	5 mL
	Prepared mustard	1 tsp.	5 mL
	Cold cooked rice	1 cup	250 mL
2.	Finely chopped deli turkey breast slices	1/3 cup	75 mL
	Finely grated peeled carrot	2 tbsp.	30 mL
	Finely grated unpeeled English cucumber	2 tbsp.	30 mL
3.	Ice cream cones (flat-bottom)	2	2

1. Put first 4 ingredients into bowl. Stir. Add rice. Mix well.
2. Add next 3 ingredients. Stir.
3. Fill cones with rice mixture, packing down gently. Pack ice cream scoop with rice mixture. Place scoop on top of rice mixture in cone. Repeat with the remaining rice mixture and cone. Makes 2 fun snacks.

1 serving: 314 Calories; 15.0 g Total Fat (8.1 g Mono, 4.9 g Poly, 1.1 g Sat); 17 mg Cholesterol; 37 g Carbohydrate; 1 g Fibre; 7 g Protein; 440 mg Sodium

Pictured on page 23.

Q: What is green and goes to a summer camp?

A: A Brussels' scout.

Lickety-Split Sundae

This super sundae's not just for Sundays—eat it any day of the week!

Get It Together: sharp knife, cutting board, liquid measures, dry measures, ice cream scoop, small cereal bowl, small bowl, mixing spoon

1.	**Medium banana**	1/2	1/2
2.	**Applesauce, chilled**	1/2 cup	125 mL
	Canned fruit cocktail, drained	1/4 cup	60 mL
3.	**Vanilla frozen yogurt**	1/2 cup	125 mL
4.	**Maraschino cherry**	1	1

1. Cut banana into 4 long pieces. Arrange banana pieces standing up against sides of cereal bowl.

2. Put applesauce and fruit cocktail into small bowl. Mix well. Spoon half of applesauce mixture into cereal bowl.

3. Spoon half of frozen yogurt over top. Repeat with remaining applesauce and frozen yogurt.

4. Place cherry on top. Eat immediately. Makes 1 stunning sundae.

1 serving: 327 Calories; 5.0 g Total Fat (trace Mono, 0.1 g Poly, 3.1 g Sat); 15 mg Cholesterol; 70 g Carbohydrate; 4 g Fibre; 4 g Protein; 53 mg Sodium

Pictured below.

Lickety-Split Sundae, above

25

Left: Bumpy Peanut Butter Balls, below Right: Yum-Yum Yogurt Layers, page 27

Bumpy Peanut Butter Balls

Don't go bowling with these bumpy balls—eat them instead!

Get It Together: dry measures, measuring spoons, small bowl, mixing spoon, small plate

1.	Crunchy peanut butter	1/4 cup	60 mL
	Liquid honey	2 tbsp.	30 mL
	Skim milk powder	2 tbsp.	30 mL
	Graham cracker crumbs	1/3 cup	75 mL
2.	Medium sweetened coconut	2 tbsp.	30 mL

1. Put first 3 ingredients into bowl. Stir. Add graham cracker crumbs. Mix well. Divide peanut butter mixture into 4 equal portions. Roll portions between your hands to make balls.

2. Spread coconut on plate. Roll balls in coconut until coated. Makes 4 sweet treats, enough for you and a pal to share.

1 serving: 365 Calories; 18.9 g Total Fat (8.5 g Mono, 5.3 g Poly, 4.2 g Sat); 1 mg Cholesterol; 41 g Carbohydrate; 3 g Fibre; 12 g Protein; 292 mg Sodium

Pictured above.

Mix It!

Yum-Yum Yogurt Layers

Be a layer slayer and devour this sweet treat made with cookies, fruit and almonds.

Get It Together: sharp knife, cutting board, measuring spoons, liquid measures, dry measures, tall glass, small bowl, mixing spoon

1.	**Chocolate chip cookies**	2	2
2.	**Berry yogurt**	1/2 cup	125 mL
	Sliced natural almonds	1 tbsp.	15 mL
3.	**Banana slices, about 1/4 inch (6 mm) thick**	6	6
	Sliced fresh strawberries	1/2 cup	125 mL

1. Break cookies into small pieces. Put into glass.
2. Put yogurt and almonds into bowl. Mix well. Spoon half of yogurt mixture over broken cookies.
3. Put 3 banana slices on top of yogurt. Put half of strawberries on top of banana slices. Repeat layers 1 more time with remaining yogurt mixture, banana slices and strawberries. Makes 1 tasty treat.

1 serving: *293 Calories; 9.1 g Total Fat (2.0 g Mono, 0.9 g Poly, 2.3 g Sat); 13 mg Cholesterol; 49 g Carbohydrate; 3 g Fibre; 6 g Protein; 102 mg Sodium*

Pictured on front cover and on page 26.

Creampuff Tip: Try using your favourite flavour of yogurt. Also, try experimenting with different kinds of nuts and fruits.

Q: What do you call cheese that doesn't belong to you?

A: Nacho cheese.

Boastin' Toastin' Choco-Treats

You'll have lots to boast about when you make these chocolatey sweet waffle treats piled high with strawberries and bananas.

Get It Together: measuring spoons, dry measures, sharp knife, cutting board, 2 serving plates, small bowl, fork, mixing spoon, table knife

1.	Cream cheese, softened	3 tbsp.	50 mL
	Prepared chocolate frosting	1/3 cup	75 mL
2.	Frozen waffles	2	2
3.	Sliced fresh strawberries	1/2 cup	125 mL
	Sliced banana	1/4 cup	60 mL

1. Put cream cheese into bowl. Mash with fork until smooth. Add frosting. Mix well.
2. Toast waffles. Place on plates. Spread frosting mixture on waffles.
3. Arrange strawberries and banana slices on top. Makes enough for you and a friend.

1 serving: 382 Calories; 18.7 g Total Fat (4.2 g Mono, 1.1 g Poly, 8.6 g Sat); 33 mg Cholesterol; 52 g Carbohydrate; 2 g Fibre; 5 g Protein; 379 mg Sodium

Pictured on page 29.

Creampuff Tip: To soften cream cheese, let it sit on the counter for about 30 minutes.

If you don't have waffles, use toasted bread instead.

The Tower Of Trifle

The goodies are piled high in this sweet treat with cake, pudding, strawberries and bananas. Use any kind of cake you like.

Get It Together: sharp knife, cutting board, liquid measures, dry measures, 2 small bowls, mixing spoon, whisk, 2 tall glasses, spoons

1.	Sliced banana	1/2 cup	125 mL
	Sliced fresh strawberries	1/2 cup	125 mL
2.	Milk	1 cup	250 mL
	Instant chocolate pudding powder (half of 4-serving size box)	1/3 cup	75 mL

(continued on next page)

Mix It!

| 3. | Small cake cubes | 1 cup | 250 mL |
| | Frozen whipped topping, thawed | 1/2 cup | 125 mL |

1. Put banana and strawberries into 1 bowl. Stir. Set aside.

2. Put milk and pudding powder into other bowl. Stir with whisk for about 2 minutes until mixture is smooth and thick.

3. Put half of cake cubes into each glass. Spoon pudding mixture over cake. Spoon fruit mixture over pudding mixture. Spoon whipped topping on top. Makes 2 towering treats.

1 serving: 320 Calories; 8.7 g Total Fat (0.9 g Mono, 0.8 g Poly, 6.0 g Sat); 10 mg Cholesterol; 56 g Carbohydrate; 3 g Fibre; 6 g Protein; 531 mg Sodium

Pictured below.

Left: Boastin' Toastin' Choco-Treats, page 28   Right: The Tower Of Trifle, page 28

Toss It!

Tossing is a form of mixing—but it has way more pizzazz! When you toss food you can do it in a plastic baggie or you can do it by gently lifting and turning food with spoons. But don't go all crazy and start tossing things on the ceiling—this is a delicate procedure!

find 19 fruits

```
E  A  Y  R  R  E  H  C  Z  Q  N  U  Y  V  R
A  G  P  V  B  L  U  E  B  E  R  R  Y  H  A
T  N  N  P  M  Z  P  N  D  E  R  H  U  R  N
I  L  O  A  L  A  Q  J  M  E  L  B  W  F  A
E  M  N  L  R  E  J  I  B  W  A  I  A  X  N
A  G  R  G  E  O  L  N  N  R  K  W  Q  M  A
O  P  U  A  Y  M  A  B  B  D  D  I  E  H  B
H  C  R  Q  E  R  R  M  U  L  P  K  N  P  Z
G  R  L  I  C  P  P  E  A  C  H  X  I  P  N
B  X  A  Y  C  P  B  J  T  P  X  U  R  U  U
Y  H  N  D  M  O  E  P  R  A  M  O  A  M  L
T  T  C  R  R  M  T  T  E  Z  W  G  T  P  E
Q  I  Y  R  R  E  B  W  A  R  T  S  C  K  M
O  U  N  L  X  X  Z  U  V  L  P  N  E  I  O
L  K  L  Y  J  G  F  B  E  Q  Y  I  N  N  N
```

APPLE	APRICOT	BANANA
BLUEBERRY	CHERRY	CRANBERRY
GRAPE	KIWI	LEMON
LIME	MANGO	NECTARINE
ORANGE	PEACH	PEAR
PLUM	PUMPKIN	
STRAWBERRY	WATERMELON	

Countdown Fruit Salad

Counting, measuring and dividing are involved in this
mathematical masterpiece. Add up the ingredients and the sum
is a yummy salad. Save any leftover fruit to make smoothies or put in yogurt.

Get It Together: sharp knife, cutting board, measuring spoons,
medium bowl, mixing spoons, small cup

1.	**Seedless grapes**	10	10
	Banana slices	9	9
	Pecan halves	8	8
	Cantaloupe cubes	7	7
	Cheddar cheese cubes	6	6
2.	**Orange segments**	5	5
	Apple slices	4	4
	Sweetened shredded coconut	3 tbsp.	50 mL
3.	**Frozen concentrated orange juice, thawed**	2 tbsp.	30 mL
	Water	1 tbsp.	15 mL

1. Put first 5 ingredients into bowl.

2. Cut each orange segment into 3 pieces. Add to fruit mixture. Cut each apple slice into 4 pieces. Add to fruit mixture. Sprinkle coconut over top. Use mixing spoons to toss fruit mixture.

3. Put concentrated orange juice and water into cup. Stir. Drizzle over fruit mixture. Toss. Makes about 2 cups (500 mL)—the perfect amount for sharing with a friend.

1 serving: 248 Calories; 12.0 g Total Fat (3.1 g Mono, 1.6 g Poly, 5.1 g Sat); 11 mg Cholesterol; 34 g Carbohydrate; 4 g Fibre; 5 g Protein; 93 mg Sodium

Pictured below.

Countdown Fruit Salad, above

Mix-Master Snacks-A-Lot

You'll be the master mixer with this sweet and salty snack.

Get It Together: dry measures, measuring spoons, medium bowl, mixing spoons

1. | Small pretzels | 1 cup | 250 mL |
    | "O"-shaped toasted oat cereal | 1/2 cup | 125 mL |
    | Honey-roasted almonds | 1/4 cup | 60 mL |
    | Candy-coated chocolates | 2 tbsp. | 30 mL |
    | Raisins | 2 tbsp. | 30 mL |

1. Put all 5 ingredients into bowl. Use mixing spoons to toss until combined. Makes about 2 cups (500 mL)—enough for 2 snacks.

1 serving: 496 Calories; 20.1 g Total Fat (9.5 g Mono, 2.7 g Poly, 7.2 g Sat); 6 mg Cholesterol; 73 g Carbohydrate; 5 g Fibre; 9 g Protein; 640 mg Sodium

Pictured on page 33.

 **Monsieur Auk-Auk Tip:** If you can't find honey-roasted almonds, use honey-roasted peanuts instead.

Cannibals won't eat clowns—they taste funny.

Toss It!

Left: Ham & Corn Feed Bag, below Right: Mix-Master Snacks-A-Lot, page 32

Ham & Corn Feed Bag

Your salad's in the bag. Make it in the bag and eat it out
of the bag—talk about easy cleanup!

Get It Together: sharp knife, cutting board, dry measures, measuring
spoons, resealable sandwich bag

1.			
Frozen kernel corn, thawed	1/3 cup	75 mL
Diced ham	1/4 cup	60 mL
Frozen peas, thawed	1/4 cup	60 mL
Cherry tomatoes, halved	3	3
Croutons	2 tbsp.	30 mL
Ranch dressing	1 tbsp.	15 mL
Chili powder, sprinkle		

1. Put all 7 ingredients into bag. Seal bag. Toss until coated. Makes about
1 cup (250 mL)—enough for 1 kid.

1 serving: 245 Calories; 11.9 g Total Fat (0.9 g Mono, 0.3 g Poly, 1.3 g Sat); 18 mg Cholesterol;
22 g Carbohydrate; 4 g Fibre; 15 g Protein; 122 mg Sodium

Pictured above.

Toss It!

Bronco Bull Eggs

Didn't think bulls laid eggs? Well, they don't but we figured if you crossed an ornery bull and a chicken, you might end up with this spicy egg spread!

Get It Together: sharp knife, cutting board, measuring spoons, small bowl, mixing spoons

1.	**Large hard-cooked egg, chopped**	1	1
	Ranch dressing	1 tbsp.	15 mL
	Hot pepper sauce	1/4 tsp.	1 mL
2.	**Crackers**	4	4

1. Put first 3 ingredients into bowl. Use mixing spoons to toss until coated.
2. Spoon egg mixture onto crackers. Makes 4 cracker snacks for you to enjoy.

1 serving: 203 Calories; 14.5 g Total Fat (2.9 g Mono, 0.9 g Poly, 3.0 g Sat); 216 mg Cholesterol; 10 g Carbohydrate; trace Fibre; 8 g Protein; 365 mg Sodium

Pictured on page 35.

Monsieur Auk-Auk Tip: Do you know how to cook the perfect hard-cooked egg? First place an egg in a small saucepan. Add cold water until about 1 inch (2.5 cm) above the egg. Bring to a boil on medium-high. Remove the saucepan from the heat. Cover with lid. Wait for 20 minutes. Drain. Cover the egg with cold water. Change the water each time it warms up until the egg is cool. Remove the shell. There you have it—the perfect hard-cooked egg!

Q: What did the spoon say to the knife?

A: Lookin' sharp.

Tomato Tossle

Like Italian food? If you do, you'll love this tomato-tossed snack!

Get It Together: sharp knife, cutting board, dry measures, grater, measuring spoons, small bowl, mixing spoons

1.			
Chopped tomato	1/3 cup	75 mL
Grated mozzarella cheese	2 tbsp.	30 mL
Fresh basil leaf, torn into small pieces	1	1
(or 1/8 tsp., 0.5 mL, dried basil)		
Olive (or cooking) oil	1/2 tsp.	2 mL
Granulated sugar	1/4 tsp.	1 mL
Garlic powder, sprinkle		
Salt, sprinkle		
2. Bread slice, toasted	1	1

1. Put first 7 ingredients into bowl. Use mixing spoons to toss until combined.

2. Cut toast into 4 pieces. Spoon tomato mixture over toast pieces. Drain remaining juice in bottom of bowl. Makes 4 tossles for you to taste.

1 serving: *143 Calories; 6.5 g Total Fat (2.8 g Mono, 0.9 g Poly, 2.4 g Sat); 12 mg Cholesterol; 16 g Carbohydrate; 1 g Fibre; 5 g Protein; 192 mg Sodium*

Pictured below.

Top: Tomato Tossle, above Bottom: Bronco Bull Eggs, page 34

Luau Wow-Wow

Who cares if you're not on a beach in Hawaii? Make your own mini-luau with this sweet and crunchy pineapple salad.

Get It Together: can opener, sharp knife, cutting board, dry measures, vegetable peeler, grater, measuring spoons, small bowl, mixing spoons, 2 cereal bowls

1.			
Canned pineapple tidbits, drained	1/2 cup	125 mL
Chopped celery	1/2 cup	125 mL
Grated peeled carrot	1/2 cup	125 mL
Raisins	1/4 cup	60 mL
Mayonnaise	2 tbsp.	30 mL
Pineapple juice	1 tsp.	5 mL

1. Put all 6 ingredients into small bowl. Use mixing spoons to toss until coated. Spoon into cereal bowls. Makes about 1 1/2 cups (375 mL)—enough for a 2-kid luau.

1 serving: 179 Calories; 7.4 g Total Fat (4.0 g Mono, 2.5 g Poly, 0.6 g Sat); 4 mg Cholesterol; 29 g Carbohydrate; 3 g Fibre; 2 g Protein; 138 mg Sodium

Pictured on page 37.

Take 1–It's A Wrap!

This chicken wrap tastes just like Chinese takeout!

Get It Together: sharp knife, cutting board, dry measures, measuring spoons, small bowl, mixing spoons, plate

1.	Chopped or torn lettuce, lightly packed	1 cup	250 mL
	Sesame ginger dressing	2 tbsp.	30 mL
2.	Flour tortilla (9 inch, 22 cm, diameter)	1	1
	Chopped cooked chicken	1/2 cup	125 mL
	Dry chow mein noodles	2 tbsp.	30 mL
3.	Sesame ginger dressing	2 tbsp.	30 mL

1. Put lettuce into bowl. Add first amount of dressing. Use mixing spoons to toss until coated. Set aside.

(continued on next page)

Toss It!

2. Place tortilla on plate. Spoon chicken in a line across middle of tortilla, leaving a small edge uncovered on both sides. Sprinkle noodles over chicken. Spoon lettuce mixture over noodles. Fold small edges over filling. Roll up from bottom to enclose filling. Cut tortilla in half.

3. Serve with second amount of dressing for dipping. Makes 1 totally wrapped up snack.

1 serving: 654 Calories; 34.5 g Total Fat (5.6 g Mono, 3.6 g Poly, 6.2 g Sat); 66 mg Cholesterol; 54 g Carbohydrate; 3 g Fibre; 29 g Protein; 1044 mg Sodium

Pictured below.

Top: Luau Wow-Wow, page 36 Bottom: Take 1—It's A Wrap!, page 36

Hickory Sticks Coleslaw

Hickory sticks may be good on their own but they're a sure hit in coleslaw!

Get It Together: measuring spoons, sharp knife, cutting board, dry measures, small bowl, mixing spoons

1. Sour cream — 2 tbsp. — 30 mL
   Water — 2 tsp. — 10 mL
   White vinegar — 2 tsp. — 10 mL
   Granulated sugar — 1 tsp. — 5 mL
   Chopped fresh dill — 1/2 tsp. — 2 mL
   (or 1/8 tsp., 0.5 mL, dried dillweed)
   Cooking oil — 1/4 tsp. — 1 mL
   Salt, sprinkle
   Pepper, sprinkle

2. Coleslaw mix — 1/2 cup — 125 mL
   Diced marble cheese — 1/4 cup — 60 mL
   Hickory sticks — 1/4 cup — 60 mL

1. Put first 8 ingredients into bowl. Stir.
2. Add remaining 3 ingredients. Use mixing spoons to toss until coated. Serve immediately. Makes about 2/3 cup (150 mL)—a fun snack for 1.

1 serving: 278 Calories; 18.9 g Total Fat (4.8 g Mono, 0.8 g Poly, 9.3 g Sat); 42 mg Cholesterol; 18 g Carbohydrate; 2 g Fibre; 10 g Protein; 213 mg Sodium

Pictured below.

Left: Hickory Sticks Coleslaw, above Right: Turkey-Lurkey Happy Wraps, page 39

Turkey-Lurkey Happy Wraps

Made with rice paper, this wrap sure is different! You'll be happy you made it. Good on its own or try with 4 O'Clock Fiesta Salsa, page 16, or Confusing Dip, page 16.

Get It Together: grater, vegetable peeler, dry measures, measuring spoons, small bowl, mixing spoons, pie plate, 2 plates, plastic wrap

1. | | | |
|---|---|---|
| **Cooked rice** | 1 cup | 250 mL |
| **Grated peeled carrot** | 1/4 cup | 60 mL |
| **Grated unpeeled English cucumber** | 1/4 cup | 60 mL |
| **Raisins** | 1/4 cup | 60 mL |
| **Mayonnaise** | 2 tbsp. | 30 mL |
| **Salt** | 1/4 tsp. | 1 mL |
| **Pepper** | 1/8 tsp. | 0.5 mL |

2. **Very warm water**

3. **Rice paper rounds**   4   4
       (6 inch, 15 cm, diameter)

4. **Thin deli turkey breast slices**   4   4

1. Put first 7 ingredients into bowl. Use mixing spoons to toss until coated.

2. Pour very warm water (as hot as you can handle) into pie plate until about 1/2 inch (12 mm) deep.

3. Dip 1 rice paper round into water for about 30 seconds until softened. Place rice paper on 1 plate.

4. Place 1 turkey slice on rice paper round. Spoon about 1/3 cup (75 mL) rice mixture onto centre of turkey slice. Spread rice in a line across middle of turkey slice, leaving a small edge uncovered on both sides. Fold small edges of rice paper round over filling. Roll up from bottom to enclose filling. Place, seam-side down, on other plate. Cover with plastic wrap. Repeat with remaining rice paper rounds, turkey slices and rice mixture. Makes 4 wraps—enough for 2 hungry kids.

1 serving: 629 Calories; 8.6 g Total Fat (4.2 g Mono, 2.6 g Poly, 1.4 g Sat); 14 mg Cholesterol; 124 g Carbohydrate; 2 g Fibre; 14 g Protein; 2007 mg Sodium

Pictured on page 38.

Zap It!

Now you're cooking! In this chapter you're dealing with hot stuff, but there's one thing to keep in mind—microwaves come in many different powers. Some cook very fast, others take a little bit longer. We tested our recipes in a 900 Watt microwave and that's how we determined our cooking times. If your microwave has more power, you need to keep an eye on your food so it doesn't overcook. If your microwave has less power, you may need to cook your food a little longer than our recommended time.

18 things you find in a kitchen

```
I   N   A   W   A   K   P   S   B   D   J   B   B   D   E
K   C   Q   L   N   L   T   N   I   M   J   A   Z   G   S
N   F   E   I   U   N   K   S   I   H   W   K   D   M   P
I   H   F   C   E   T   H   U   M   B   T   I   C   S   O
S   E   A   V   R   W   A   B   D   H   R   N   P   E   O
Q   N   O   V   A   E   R   P   O   F   X   G   A   P   N
G   L   A   S   S   D   A   E   S   W   T   S   N   R   H
Y   Y   H   X   P   H   P   M   X   Q   L   H   R   E   K
W   E   F   O   R   K   Y   L   S   I   D   E   E   T   K
R   H   T   P   U   C   N   Y   A   C   M   E   N   S   R
N   Y   V   Z   W   G   C   Y   A   T   O   T   W   A   J
B   B   T   T   W   Z   I   F   K   C   E   O   Z   O   L
D   S   C   O   T   B   I   S   V   T   F   K   P   T   X
E   J   G   V   F   X   N   I   B   S   Q   Q   F   Z   T
E   V   A   W   O   R   C   I   M   Z   O   K   L   C   V
```

BAKING SHEET	BOWL	CUP
DISHWASHER	FORK	FRIDGE
GLASS	ICE CREAM SCOOP	KNIFE
MICROWAVE	MIXER	OVEN
PAN	PLATE	POT
SINK	SPATULA	SPOON

The Great Apple & Cheese Squeeze, below

The Great Apple & Cheese Squeeze

Put the squeeze on hunger with this apple and cheese-filled snack.

Get It Together: grater, measuring spoons, dry measures, sharp knife, cutting board, microwave-safe plate

1. | | | |
    |---|---|---|
    | **Flour tortilla (6 inch, 15 cm, diameter)** | 1 | 1 |
    | **Grated medium Cheddar cheese** | 2 tbsp. | 30 mL |
    | **Thinly sliced apple** | 1/3 cup | 75 mL |
    | **Grated medium Cheddar cheese** | 2 tbsp. | 30 mL |

1. Place tortilla on plate. Sprinkle first amount of cheese on 1 half of tortilla. Arrange apple over cheese. Sprinkle second amount of cheese over top. Fold uncovered side of tortilla over filling. Press down lightly. Microwave on high (100%) for about 30 seconds until cheese is melted. Cut tortilla in half. Makes enough for 1 kid.

1 serving: 226 Calories; 11.5 g Total Fat (3.8 g Mono, 0.6 g Poly, 6.5 g Sat); 30 mg Cholesterol; 21 g Carbohydrate; 1 g Fibre; 10 g Protein; 314 mg Sodium

Pictured above.

Fruit Island

You certainly won't go hungry if you're ever stranded on this island!

Get It Together: sharp knife, cutting board, dry measures, measuring spoons, liquid measures, small microwave-safe dish, mixing spoon, 2 small bowls

1.	Mixed dried fruit, chopped	1/4 cup	60 mL
	Apple juice	1 tbsp.	15 mL
	Water	1 tbsp.	15 mL
2.	Vanilla yogurt	1 cup	250 mL

1. Put first 3 ingredients into dish. Microwave, covered, on high (100%) for 1 minute. Stir. Microwave, uncovered, on high (100%) for another 30 to 60 seconds until fruit is soft and liquid is evaporated. Stir.

2. Spoon yogurt into bowls. Spoon half of fruit mixture in centre of each bowl. Makes 2 tasty snacks.

1 serving: 138 Calories; 1.5 g Total Fat (0 g Mono, 0 g Poly, 1.3 g Sat); 10 mg Cholesterol; 23 g Carbohydrate; 1 g Fibre; 6 g Protein; 113 mg Sodium

Pictured on page 43.

Cookbot 3000 Tip: There are many varieties of mixed dried fruit. Are you in the mood for mango mania, sweet papaya, sticky pineapple or tart cranberries? Mix it up as much as you like, just make sure you keep the amount the same.

Buffoon's Macaroons

You won't find an easier way to make these chewy chocolate treats.

Get It Together: dry measures, measuring spoons, medium bowl, small bowl, whisk, mixing spoon, parchment paper, scissors, 2 microwave-safe dinner plates

1.	Egg white product (or 1 egg white)	2 tbsp.	30 mL
2.	Icing (confectioner's) sugar	1/3 cup	75 mL
	Cocoa, sifted if lumpy	1 tsp.	5 mL
3.	Medium unsweetened coconut	3/4 cup	175 mL

(continued on next page)

Zap It!

1. Put egg white into medium bowl. Beat with the whisk until bubbly on top.

2. Put icing sugar and cocoa into small bowl. Stir. Add to egg white. Mix well.

3. Add coconut. Stir. Cut two 6 inch (15 cm) pieces of parchment paper. Place a parchment sheet on each plate. Using a rounded tablespoon of coconut mixture for each, spoon 4 mounds onto each sheet. Make sure the mounds are spaced about 1 1/2 inches (3.8 cm) apart. Place 1 plate in the microwave. Microwave on high (100%) for about 90 seconds until the mixture is firm. Remove the plate from the microwave. Let cool for 5 minutes. Repeat with the second plate. Makes 8 macaroons—enough to share if you're feeling generous.

1 serving: 271 Calories; 18.0 g Total Fat (0.8 g Mono, 0.2 g Poly, 16.0 g Sat); 0 mg Cholesterol; 27 g Carbohydrate; 5 g Fibre; 4 g Protein; 38 mg Sodium

Pictured below.

Top: Fruit Island, page 42   Bottom: Buffoon's Macaroons, page 42

Left: Ex-Cous Me Peas, page 45 Right: Micro-Chips, below

Micro-Chips

These crisp pita chips are great for dipping!

Get It Together: measuring spoons, cutting board, pastry brush, paper towel, sharp knife

1. **Pita bread (8 inch, 20 cm, diameter)**   1   1
    Cooking oil   1/4 tsp.   1 mL

2. **Salt, sprinkle**

1. Place pita bread on cutting board. Brush cooking oil on one side of pita bread.

2. Sprinkle with salt. Cut pita bread into 8 triangles. Place paper towel in microwave. Lay pita pieces on top in a single layer. Microwave on high (100%) for 1 minute. Wait for about 2 minutes until crisp and cool enough to handle. Makes enough for 1 cyber chef.

1 serving: 175 Calories; 1.9 g Total Fat (0.7 g Mono, 0.7 g Poly, 0.2 g Sat); 0 mg Cholesterol; 33 g Carbohydrate; 1 g Fibre; 5 g Protein; 322 mg Sodium

Pictured above.

(continued on next page)

CINNAMON MICRO-CHIPS: Instead of salt, sprinkle with 1/2 tsp. (2 mL) granulated sugar and 1/8 tsp. (0.5 mL) ground cinnamon before cooking.

HERBED MICRO-CHIPS: Add a sprinkle of Italian seasoning with the salt before cooking.

SALT AND PEPPER MICRO-CHIPS: Add a sprinkle of pepper with the salt before cooking.

SEASONED MICRO-CHIPS: Instead of salt, use a sprinkle of seasoned salt before cooking.

Ex-Cous Me Peas

You don't need an excuse to try something new. Couscous is actually tiny bits of pasta—and this version is good and spicy!

Get It Together: measuring spoons, liquid measures, dry measures, grater, small microwave-safe bowl, mixing spoon, fork

1.	Prepared chicken broth	1/4 cup	60 mL
	Chunky salsa	2 tbsp.	30 mL
	Frozen peas	2 tbsp.	30 mL
	Chili powder	1/8 tsp.	0.5 mL
2.	Couscous	1/4 cup	60 mL
3.	Grated mild Cheddar cheese	1 tbsp.	15 mL

1. Put first 4 ingredients into bowl. Stir. Microwave, covered, on high (100%) for about 2 minutes until boiling.

2. Add couscous. Stir. Cover with lid. Wait for about 5 minutes until couscous is tender and liquid is soaked up. Stir with fork.

3. Sprinkle cheese over top. Cover with lid. Wait for about 1 minute until cheese is melted. Makes about 1 cup (250 mL)—enough for 1 kid.

1 serving: 232 Calories; 3.0 g Total Fat (0.8 g Mono, 0.3 g Poly, 1.6 g Sat); 7 mg Cholesterol; 41 g Carbohydrate; 3 g Fibre; 9 g Protein; 652 mg Sodium

Pictured on page 44.

Sea Wolf BBQ Sub

Are you hungry enough to wolf down this saucy meatball sub? If you have a leftover hamburger, cut it into pieces and use it instead of meatballs.

Get It Together: measuring spoons, grater, dry measures, sharp knife, cutting board, table knife, microwave-safe plate, paper towel

1.	Barbecue sauce	2 tbsp.	30 mL
	Submarine bun (8 inch, 20 cm), split	1	1
	Grated medium Cheddar cheese	1/3 cup	75 mL
	Refried beans	2 tbsp.	30 mL
2.	Lettuce leaf	1	1
	Dill pickle, sliced	1	1
3.	Frozen (or leftover) cooked meatballs	5	5
4.	Barbecue sauce	2 tbsp.	30 mL

1. Spread barbecue sauce on top half of submarine bun. Sprinkle cheese over barbecue sauce. Spread refried beans on bottom half of submarine bun.

2. Place lettuce over refried beans. Arrange pickle slices over lettuce.

3. Place meatballs on plate. Cover loosely with paper towel. Microwave on high (100%) for about 2 minutes until meatballs are hot. Cut meatballs in half. Arrange meatball halves over pickle slices. Place the other half of submarine bun over meatballs, cheese-side down.

4. Serve with second amount of barbecue sauce for dipping. Makes 1 submarine sandwich—enough to feed 2 hungry sea cadets.

1 serving: 396 Calories; 17.8 g Total Fat (6.5 g Mono, 1.7 g Poly, 7.8 g Sat); 79 mg Cholesterol; 35 g Carbohydrate; 4 g Fibre; 23 g Protein; 1497 mg Sodium

Pictured on page 47.

Cookbot 3000 Tip: Store the remaining refried beans in an airtight container in the fridge for up to 1 week, or freeze in smaller amounts to use in other recipes.

Top: Sea Wolf BBQ Sub, above
Bottom: Folded Pizza Subwich, page 48

Zap It!

Folded Pizza Subwich

Tastes like a pizza and looks like one too—until you fold it over and it becomes a sub!

Get It Together: measuring spoons, sharp knife, cutting board, grater, dry measures, microwave-safe plate, spoon

1.	Pizza sauce	2 tbsp.	30 mL
	Hot dog bun, split	1	1
2.	Pepperoni slices	3	3
	Thinly sliced red pepper rings, cut in half	3	3
	Grated medium Cheddar cheese	1/2 cup	125 mL

1. Spread pizza sauce on bun halves. Place them, side-by-side, on plate.
2. Arrange pepperoni slices over sauce. Arrange red pepper over pepperoni. Sprinkle with cheese. Microwave on high (100%) for about 1 minute until cheese is melted. Let cool for 3 minutes. Place 1 bun half on top of other, cheese-sides facing each other, to make a sandwich. Makes 1 really tasty subwich.

1 serving: 531 Calories; 35.6 g Total Fat (12.8 g Mono, 3.0 g Poly, 17.7 g Sat); 85 mg Cholesterol; 26 g Carbohydrate; 2 g Fibre; 26 g Protein; 1360 mg Sodium

Pictured on page 47.

Space Pod Soup

Green space pods float in a galaxy of chicken noodle soup!

Get It Together: liquid measures, sharp knife, cutting board, dry measures, medium microwave-safe bowl, mixing spoon, ladle, 2 soup bowls

1.	Package of instant noodles with chicken seasoning packet	3 oz.	85 g
	Water	2 cups	500 mL
2.	Sugar snap peas, trimmed and cut in half	3/4 cup	175 mL
	Diced cooked chicken	1/2 cup	125 mL

(continued on next page)

Zap It!

1. Break noodles into 6 pieces. Put them into medium bowl. Set seasoning packet aside. Pour water over noodles. Microwave, covered, on high (100%) for 3 minutes. Stir.

2. Add peas and chicken. Stir. Microwave, covered, on high (100%) for about 2 minutes until peas start to soften. Add seasoning packet. Stir. Spoon into soup bowls. Makes about 3 cups (750 mL)—enough for 2 hungry astronauts.

1 serving: 230 Calories; 3.1 g Total Fat (0.9 g Mono, 0.6 g Poly, 0.7 g Sat); 31 mg Cholesterol; 31 g Carbohydrate; 2 g Fibre; 18 g Protein; 490 mg Sodium

Pictured below.

Cookbot 3000 Tip: Not sure how to trim sugar snap peas? It's easy! Just snap or break the stem end of the pea and pull the string that comes with it all the way down the length of the pea. Throw the stringy part away.

Space Pod Soup, page 48

Fry It!

Hear that sizzle? You will soon! Get your frying pan and your pancake lifter ready and you're good-to-go.

> **Q1:** Why did the tomato turn red?
>
> **Q2:** What kind of soda would you never drink?

Answers: **Q1:** It saw salad dressing **Q2:** Baking soda

50

Hit-The-Trail Mix

Has your get-up-and-go got-up-and-went? Give yourself enough energy to make it through to dinnertime with this fruit and nut mix.

Get It Together: dry measures, measuring spoons, small frying pan, wooden spoon, small bowl

1.	Whole natural almonds	1/4 cup	60 mL
2.	Unsalted sunflower seeds	2 tbsp.	30 mL
3.	Dried papaya chunks	1/4 cup	60 mL
	Dried pineapple chunks	1/4 cup	60 mL
	Raisins	1/4 cup	60 mL

1. Put almonds into frying pan. Heat and stir with wooden spoon on medium for 3 to 4 minutes until lightly browned. Transfer almonds to bowl.

2. Put sunflower seeds into same frying pan. Heat and stir on medium for 1 to 2 minutes until golden. Add to almonds.

3. Add remaining 3 ingredients to almond mixture. Stir. Let cool for 5 minutes. Makes about 1 1/2 cups (375 mL)—enough for 2 happy campers.

1 serving: 325 Calories; 13.4 g Total Fat (6.6 g Mono, 4.9 g Poly, 1.2 g Sat); 0 mg Cholesterol; 51 g Carbohydrate; 8 g Fibre; 7 g Protein; 15 mg Sodium

Pictured below.

Creampuff Tip: If you can't find dried papaya chunks, use dried mango, apricots, dates or figs. Any one of these is a great-tasting substitution.

Hit-The-Trail Mix, above

Stir-Crazy Granola

Feeling a little bored? Well then, hop to it and stir-fry yourself some granola!

Get It Together: measuring spoons, dry measures, small frying pan, wooden spoon, plate

1. **Butter** — 1 tbsp. — 15 mL
   Sesame seeds — 2 tbsp. — 30 mL
   Honey — 1 tbsp. — 15 mL

2. **Large flake rolled oats** — 1/2 cup — 125 mL
   Sliced almonds — 2 tbsp. — 30 mL
   Medium sweetened coconut — 1 tbsp. — 15 mL
   Ground cinnamon, sprinkle

1. Melt and spread butter in frying pan on medium. Add sesame seeds and honey. Cook, stirring often with wooden spoon, for about 2 minutes until sesame seeds are golden.

2. Add remaining 4 ingredients. Cook, stirring often, for 2 to 3 minutes until oatmeal mixture is golden. Spoon oatmeal mixture onto plate. Spread out evenly with wooden spoon. Let cool for about 5 minutes until dry. Break apart larger pieces. Makes about 1 1/3 cups (325 mL) —enough for you and a stir-crazy friend.

1 serving: 261 Calories; 15.1 g Total Fat (5.1 g Mono, 2.9 g Poly, 5.1 g Sat); 15 mg Cholesterol; 26 g Carbohydrate; 4 g Fibre; 6 g Protein; 47 mg Sodium

Pictured on page 53.

Creampuff Tip: Make sure everything is measured beforehand and ready to add to the pan so the sesame seeds don't burn. Although you might be tempted to sample your creation right away, be sure to wait until it's cool so you don't burn yourself!

Q: Who grants wishes to cows?

A: Dairy godmothers.

Stir-Crazy Granola, page 52

Ham & Cheese Wafflewich

Forget the bread—ham and cheese taste so much better in a waffle sandwich!

Get It Together: measuring spoons, grater, small frying pan with lid, table knife, pancake lifter

1.	**Butter**	**2 tsp.**	**10 mL**
2.	**Prepared mustard**	**1/2 tsp.**	**2 mL**
	Slice of deli ham, cut to fit waffle	**1**	**1**
	Frozen waffles	**2**	**2**
	Grated medium Cheddar cheese	**2 tbsp.**	**30 mL**

1. Melt and spread butter in frying pan on medium.

2. Spread mustard on one side of ham. Place 1 waffle in pan. Sprinkle cheese over waffle. Place ham over cheese. Place second waffle on top of ham. Cover with lid. Cook for about 2 minutes until waffle is browned on bottom. Use lifter to check. Press top waffle with lifter so it will stick to melting cheese. Carefully turn wafflewich over. Cover with lid. Cook for another 2 minutes until both sides of wafflewich are browned and cheese is melted. Makes 1 wafflewich for 1 lucky kid.

1 serving: 335 Calories; 18.6 g Total Fat (3.3 g Mono, 0.4 g Poly, 9.3 g Sat); 65 mg Cholesterol; 30 g Carbohydrate; 1 g Fibre; 13 g Protein; 914 mg Sodium

Pictured on front cover.

Fry It!

UFO

What's that up in the sky? It's an Unidentified Frying Object! Serve this alien edible with a slice of toast or on a toasted English muffin half for a more filling snack.

Get It Together: measuring spoons, table knife, can opener, grater, small frying pan with lid, pancake lifter

1.	**Cooking oil**	1/4 tsp.	1 mL
	Deli ham slice, cut to fit pineapple slice	1	1
	Canned pineapple slice	1	1
2.	**Grated medium Cheddar cheese**	2 tbsp.	30 mL
	Pepper, sprinkle		

1. Heat cooking oil in frying pan on medium for 3 minutes. Put ham and pineapple slice in pan beside each other. Cook for about 2 minutes until both are starting to brown on bottom. Use lifter to check. Turn ham and pineapple slice over. Cook for 1 minute. Place pineapple slice on top of ham slice.

2. Sprinkle cheese and pepper over pineapple. Cover with lid. Turn down heat to medium-low. Cook for about 2 minutes until cheese is melted. Makes 1 tasty treat.

1 serving: 132 Calories; 6.1 g Total Fat (2.0 g Mono, 0.5 g Poly, 3.1 g Sat); 25 mg Cholesterol; 12 g Carbohydrate; 1 g Fibre; 8 g Protein; 398 mg Sodium

Pictured on page 55.

1. Kooky Zooky Coins, page 56
2. UFO, above
3. Cluckin' 'Za, page 57

Creampuff Tip: Keep the remaining pineapple slices in an airtight container in the refrigerator for up to 5 days. Pineapple slices make a great snack— and don't forget to drink the juice!

Fry It!

Kooky Zooky Coins

These crispy, golden zucchini coins are delicious on their own or with
4 O'Clock Fiesta Salsa, page 16.

Get It Together: dry measures, measuring spoons, sharp knife, cutting
board, large resealable freezer bag, medium bowl, whisk, mixing spoon,
plate, large frying pan, pancake lifter

1.	**Fine dry bread crumbs**	1/3 cup	75 mL
	Celery salt	1/2 tsp.	2 mL
	Pepper	1/4 tsp.	1 mL
	Ground cinnamon	1/8 tsp.	0.5 mL
2.	**Large egg**	1	1
	Unpeeled zucchini slices,	20	20
	about 1/2 inch (12 mm) thick		
3.	**Cooking oil**	2 tbsp.	30 mL

1. Put first 4 ingredients into freezer bag. Seal bag. Shake well.

2. Break egg into bowl. Beat with whisk until egg is bubbly on top.
   Add zucchini. Stir until coated. Transfer half of zucchini into bag.
   Seal bag. Shake until coated. Remove zucchini from bag and place
   on plate. Repeat with remaining zucchini and crumb mixture.

3. Heat cooking oil in frying pan on medium for 3 minutes. Arrange zucchini
   in pan in a single layer. Cook for 3 to 5 minutes until golden on bottom.
   Use lifter to check. Turn zucchini slices over. Cook for another 3 to
   5 minutes until golden on both sides. Makes 20 coins for 2 wealthy kids.

1 serving: 229 Calories; 17.1 g Total Fat (9.5 g Mono, 4.6 g Poly, 2.0 g Sat); 93 mg Cholesterol;
14 g Carbohydrate; 1 g Fibre; 5 g Protein; 436 mg Sodium

Pictured on page 55.

Q: What did one
fish say to another?

A: If we keep our
mouths closed, we
won't get caught.

Cluckin' 'Za

Just like pizza but with an egg and potato twist!

Get It Together: measuring spoons, dry measures, sharp knife, cutting board, grater, medium non-stick frying pan with lid, mixing spoon, small bowl, whisk

1.	Butter	2 tsp.	10 mL
	Frozen shredded hash brown potatoes	1/2 cup	125 mL
	Finely chopped green onion	1 tbsp.	15 mL
2.	Large egg	1	1
	Dried oregano	1/8 tsp.	0.5 mL
	Salt, sprinkle		
	Pepper, sprinkle		
3.	Deli pepperoni slices	3	3
	Grated mozzarella cheese	3 tbsp.	50 mL
4.	Pizza sauce	1 tbsp.	15 mL

1. Melt and spread butter in frying pan on medium. Add potatoes and onion. Cook for about 5 minutes, stirring occasionally, until potatoes are lightly browned. Spread potatoes evenly in pan.

2. Break egg into bowl. Beat with whisk until egg is bubbly on top. Add next 3 ingredients. Stir. Pour egg mixture evenly over potatoes in pan. Do not stir.

3. Arrange pepperoni slices over top. Sprinkle with cheese. Turn down heat to medium-low. Cover with lid. Cook for 2 to 3 minutes until cheese is melted and egg is firm. Remove pan from heat.

4. Spoon pizza sauce over top. Makes enough for 1 pizza-craving kid.

1 serving: 437 Calories; 36.9 g Total Fat (14.6 g Mono, 3.2 g Poly, 16.4 g Sat); 249 mg Cholesterol; 17 g Carbohydrate; 1 g Fibre; 19 g Protein; 960 mg Sodium

Pictured on page 55.

Q: Why do fish live in salt water?

A: Because pepper makes them sneeze.

1. Fried Funky Monkey, page 60
2. *El Queso Grande,* page 59
3. *Quelle Surprise!,* page 61

El Queso Grande

The name means "big cheese," so if you like cheese and a little spicy Mexican heat, you'll love this sandwich.

Get It Together: measuring spoons, dry measures, table knife, 2 small shallow bowls, whisk, spoon, medium frying pan with lid, pancake lifter

1.	Butter	2 tsp.	10 mL
	Bread slices	2	2
	Grated Mexican cheese blend	1/4 cup	60 mL
2.	Large egg	1	1
	Milk	2 tbsp.	30 mL
	Grated Parmesan cheese	2 tsp.	10 mL
	Pepper, sprinkle		
3.	Fine dry bread crumbs	2 tbsp.	30 mL
	Seasoned salt	1/8 tsp.	0.5 mL
4.	Butter	2 tsp.	10 mL
5.	Salsa	2 tbsp.	30 mL

1. Spread 1 tsp. (5 mL) butter on 1 side of each bread slice. Sprinkle cheese over butter on 1 bread slice. Cover with second bread slice, buttered-side down. Press down firmly on edges to seal.

2. Break egg into 1 bowl. Add milk. Beat with whisk until mixture is bubbly on top. Add Parmesan cheese and pepper. Stir. Dip both sides of sandwich into egg mixture. Let sit in egg mixture for about 2 minutes until all of egg mixture is soaked up into bread.

3. Put bread crumbs and seasoned salt into other bowl. Stir. Gently press both sides of sandwich into crumb mixture until coated.

4. Melt and spread 1 tsp. (5 mL) butter in frying pan on medium. Place sandwich in pan. Turn down heat to medium-low. Cover with lid. Cook for about 5 minutes until golden and crisp on bottom. Use lifter to check. Add remaining butter to pan. Carefully turn sandwich over. Cook for another 6 to 8 minutes until golden and crisp on both sides. Cut sandwich in half.

5. Serve sandwich with salsa for dipping. Makes a big sandwich for 1 hungry kid.

1 serving: 627 Calories; 39.6 g Total Fat (8.3 g Mono, 1.6 g Poly, 20.5 g Sat); 270 mg Cholesterol; 41 g Carbohydrate; 1 g Fibre; 28 g Protein; 1419 mg Sodium

Pictured on page 58.

Fried Funky Monkey

Fried raisin bread with banana and chocolate—does it get any better?

Get It Together: measuring spoons, sharp knife, cutting board, table knife, small frying pan, pancake lifter

1.	**Spreadable cream cheese**	1 tbsp.	15 mL
	Raisin bread slices	2	2
	Thin banana slices	10	10
	Milk chocolate chips	2 tsp.	10 mL
2.	**Butter**	2 tsp.	10 mL

1. Spread cream cheese on 1 side of each bread slice. Arrange banana slices over cream cheese on 1 bread slice. Sprinkle chocolate chips over banana slices. Cover with other bread slice, cream cheese-side down.

2. Spread 1 tsp. (5 mL) butter on top side of sandwich. Melt and spread remaining butter in frying pan on medium-low. Carefully place sandwich in pan, buttered-side up. Cook for 3 to 5 minutes until bottom is golden. Use lifter to check. Carefully turn sandwich over. Cook for another 3 to 5 minutes until both sides are golden and chocolate chips are melted. Cut sandwich into 4 pieces. Makes 1 funky monkey.

1 serving: 346 Calories; 17.2 g Total Fat (3.9 g Mono, 0.8 g Poly, 10.2 g Sat); 37 mg Cholesterol; 45 g Carbohydrate; 4 g Fibre; 6 g Protein; 313 mg Sodium

Pictured on page 58.

Creampuff Tip: Try butterscotch chips or peanut butter chips instead of chocolate chips.

Q: What do you call a book about eggs?

A: A yolk book.

Fry It!

Quelle Surprise!

The surprise in this French toast is the raspberry centre!

Get It Together: measuring spoons, small plate, fork, small bowl, whisk, shallow pie plate, large frying pan, pancake lifter, plate, knife

1.	**Cream cheese, softened**	2 tbsp.	30 mL
	Raspberry jam (not jelly)	2 tbsp.	30 mL
2.	**Large egg**	1	1
	Milk	2 tbsp.	30 mL
3.	**Butter**	2 tsp.	10 mL
	Bread slices	2	2
4.	**Icing (confectioner's) sugar**	2 tsp.	10 mL
	Ground cinnamon, sprinkle		

1. Put cream cheese and jam onto plate. Mash with fork until smooth. Set aside.

2. Break egg into small bowl. Add milk. Beat with whisk until mixture is bubbly on top. Pour into pie plate.

3. Melt and spread butter in frying pan on medium-high. Dip bread slices into egg mixture, coating both sides. Arrange bread slices in pan. Cook for 1 to 2 minutes until the bread slices are browned on bottom. Use lifter to check. Turn bread slices over. Cook for another 1 to 2 minutes until browned on both sides. Remove bread slices to plate. Spread the cream cheese mixture on 1 bread slice. Cover with remaining bread slice. Cut sandwich in half.

4. Sprinkle icing sugar and cinnamon over top. Makes 1 surprising snack.

1 serving: 515 Calories; 26.1 g Total Fat (4.1 g Mono, 1.0 g Poly, 13.7 g Sat); 239 mg Cholesterol; 60 g Carbohydrate; 0 g Fibre; 13 g Protein; 500 mg Sodium

Pictured on page 58.

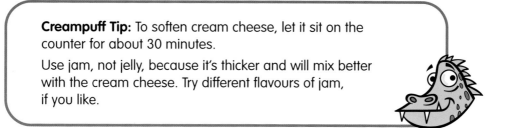

Creampuff Tip: To soften cream cheese, let it sit on the counter for about 30 minutes.

Use jam, not jelly, because it's thicker and will mix better with the cream cheese. Try different flavours of jam, if you like.

Gold Dust Flapjacks

Thar's gold in these here pancakes (well, applesauce, anyway)! Try them cold with yogurt or applesauce for a dip.

Get It Together: dry measures, liquid measures, measuring spoons, medium bowl, mixing spoon, small bowl, whisk, large frying pan, spoon, pancake lifter, serving plate, foil

1.	**Pancake mix**	1 1/4 cups	300 mL
2.	**Large egg**	1	1
	Vanilla yogurt	3/4 cup	175 mL
	Applesauce	1/2 cup	125 mL
3.	**Cooking oil**	1 tbsp.	15 mL

1. Put pancake mix into medium bowl. Dig a hole in centre of pancake mix with mixing spoon.

2. Break egg into small bowl. Beat with whisk until egg is bubbly on top. Add yogurt and applesauce. Stir well. Pour yogurt mixture into hole in pancake mix. Stir just until pancake mix is moistened. Batter will be lumpy.

3. Heat 1 tsp. (5 mL) cooking oil in frying pan on medium-low for 3 minutes. Measure batter into pan, using about 1/4 cup (60 mL) for each pancake. Use back of spoon to spread batter into a 4 inch (10 cm) wide circle. Cook for about 3 minutes until bubbles form on top and edges of pancakes look dry. Use lifter to turn pancakes over. Cook for another 2 to 3 minutes until bottoms are golden. Use lifter to check. Remove pancakes to serving plate. Cover with foil to keep warm. Repeat with remaining batter, heating more cooking oil in pan before each batch, if necessary, so pancakes won't stick. Makes 8 pancakes—a filling snack for 2 hungry kids.

1 serving: 446 Calories; 11.7 g Total Fat (5.3 g Mono, 2.9 g Poly, 2.2 g Sat); 99 mg Cholesterol; 70 g Carbohydrate; 5 g Fibre; 14 g Protein; 1009 mg Sodium

Pictured on page 64.

Creampuff Tip: Experiment a little! Make these pancakes using different flavours of applesauce and yogurt until you find the combination you like the best.

No Dud Spud Cakes

These spuds in pancake form are super easy to make—you'll never end up with a dud!

Get It Together: measuring spoons, dry measures, small bowl, whisk, large frying pan, spoon, pancake lifter

1.	**Large egg**	1	1
	Seasoned salt	1/4 tsp.	1 mL
	Pepper, sprinkle		
	Garlic powder, sprinkle		
2.	**Frozen shredded hash brown potatoes**	1 cup	250 mL
	All-purpose flour	1 tbsp.	15 mL
3.	**Cooking oil**	1 tsp.	5 mL
4.	**Ketchup**	2 tbsp.	30 mL

1. Put first 4 ingredients into bowl. Beat with whisk until mixture is bubbly on top.

2. Add potatoes. Sprinkle flour over top. Stir until potatoes are coated.

3. Heat cooking oil in frying pan on medium for 3 minutes. Spoon potato mixture into 4 mounds in pan. Flatten each mound with back of spoon. Try not to let cakes touch each other. Cook for 3 to 4 minutes until bottoms are golden. Use lifter to check. Turn cakes over. Cook for another 3 to 4 minutes until cakes are golden on both sides.

4. Serve cakes with ketchup for dipping. Makes 4 spud cakes—enough for you to share with a friend.

1 serving: 147 Calories; 9.6 g Total Fat (4.5 g Mono, 1.6 g Poly, 2.8 g Sat); 93 mg Cholesterol; 21 g Carbohydrate; 1 g Fibre; 5 g Protein; 408 mg Sodium

Pictured on page 64.

Creampuff Tip: Instead of ketchup, try other dips like sour cream or salsa.

Q: What does the invisible man drink?

A: Evaporated milk.

Fry It!

Humpty Dumpty Burrito

Don't bother trying to put Humpty Dumpty back together again—just scramble him up and serve him in a burrito! Try with your favourite salsa or with 4 O'Clock Fiesta Salsa, page 16.

Get It Together: grater, measuring spoons, liquid measures, small bowl, whisk, small frying pan with lid, plate, spoon

1.	**Large egg**	1	1
	Milk	1 tsp.	5 mL
	Salt, sprinkle		
	Pepper, sprinkle		
2.	**Butter**	1 tsp.	5 mL
3.	**Grated medium Cheddar cheese**	2 tbsp.	30 mL
4.	**Flour tortilla (6 inch, 15 cm, diameter)**	1	1
	Salsa	1/4 cup	60 mL

1. Break egg into bowl. Add next 3 ingredients. Beat with whisk until mixture is bubbly on top.

2. Melt and spread butter in frying pan on medium. Pour egg mixture into pan. Heat and stir for about 1 minute until egg mixture is almost cooked. It should still be a little soft and creamy.

3. Sprinkle cheese on top. Remove pan from heat. Cover with lid. Wait for about 1 minute until cheese is melted.

4. Place tortilla on plate. Spoon the egg mixture in a line across middle of tortilla, leaving a small edge uncovered on both sides. Fold small edges over filling. Roll up from bottom to enclose filling. Place seam-side down on plate. Serve with salsa. Makes enough for 1 spicy kid.

1 serving: 278 Calories; 15.7 g Total Fat (5.6 g Mono, 1.4 g Poly, 7.5 g Sat); 211 mg Cholesterol; 21 g Carbohydrate; 2 g Fibre; 13 g Protein; 597 mg Sodium

Pictured on page 64.

1. Gold Dust Flapjacks, page 62
2. No Dud Spud Cakes, page 63
3. Humpty Dumpty Burrito, above

Fry It!

Boil It!

They say a watched pot never boils. Put that theory to test in this chapter and have your snacks bubbling on the stovetop in no time.

find 15 flavours of ice cream

```
S  W  E  U  N  C  S  I  A  Z  G  X  U  A  X
U  T  O  L  O  I  N  C  D  T  N  Z  T  L  X
Y  T  R  F  P  O  F  B  N  C  E  Y  Q  L  H
O  R  F  A  M  A  O  I  H  C  A  T  S  I  P
P  E  R  U  W  U  M  Q  I  C  P  E  R  N  F
E  W  P  E  W  B  X  N  H  B  O  D  F  A  M
Z  S  I  U  B  L  E  O  W  N  L  E  B  V  H
H  C  A  E  P  P  C  R  V  N  I  M  U  G  O
M  L  X  A  A  O  S  O  R  I  T  I  C  C  H
E  G  D  T  L  Z  J  A  C  Y  A  L  N  A  T
X  E  M  A  A  Y  X  D  R  O  N  V  O  R  C
Q  D  T  R  A  I  N  B  O  W  N  F  L  A  W
B  E  A  U  A  M  M  M  S  C  V  U  D  M  F
Q  F  C  A  G  O  X  O  F  F  H  E  T  E  Y
J  B  N  E  E  R  Z  H  O  K  K  H  A  L  U
```

CARAMEL
COFFEE
MINT
PISTACHIO
SPUMONI

CHOCOLATE
LIME
NEAPOLITAN
RAINBOW
STRAWBERRY

COCONUT
MAPLE
PEACH
RASPBERRY
VANILLA

Don't Box Me In Pudding

Pudding doesn't come from a box! This is how real chefs make it. If you want to eat this cold, cover with plastic wrap that touches the top of the pudding, and refrigerate for 2 hours.

Get It Together: liquid measures, measuring spoons, small dish, mixing spoon, small saucepan, 2 cereal bowls

1.	Mashed overripe banana	1/4 cup	60 mL
	Lemon juice	1/4 tsp.	1 mL
2.	Egg yolk (large)	1	1
	Milk	3/4 cup	175 mL
	Granulated sugar	2 tbsp.	30 mL
	Cornstarch	4 tsp.	20 mL
3.	Butter	1 tsp.	5 mL
4.	Chocolate chips	1 tbsp.	15 mL
	Banana chips	4	4

1. Put banana and lemon juice into dish. Mix well.

2. Put next 4 ingredients into saucepan. Mix well. Cook on medium for about 5 minutes, stirring constantly, until mixture starts to boil and thicken. Add banana mixture. Stir. Cook for about 1 minute, stirring constantly, until mixture is boiling. Cook and stir for 1 minute. Remove pan from heat.

3. Add butter to banana mixture. Stir until melted. Wait for about 5 minutes, stirring occasionally, until slightly cooled. Spoon into bowls.

4. Top each bowl of pudding with half of chocolate chips and banana chips. Makes about 1 cup (250 mL)—enough for 2 kids to enjoy.

1 serving: 245 Calories; 9.2 g Total Fat (1.1 g Mono, 0.4 g Poly, 4.4 g Sat); 107 mg Cholesterol; 36 g Carbohydrate; 1 g Fibre; 5 g Protein; 66 mg Sodium

Pictured on page 68.

Monsieur Auk-Auk Tip: If you don't have an egg separator, you can separate the yolk from the egg white by cracking the egg as close to the middle as possible, being careful not to break the yolk. Hold the half of the shell with the yolk in it in one hand and the other half of the shell in the other hand. Allow as much of the egg white as possible to run out of the shell and into a small bowl. Then, transfer the yolk to the other half of the shell, allowing more of the egg white to run out. Repeat, a few times, until most of the egg white has been removed.

Rock-A-Hula Sauce

This rockin' sweet pineapple sauce is great on pancakes, waffles, yogurt or ice cream.

Get It Together: can opener, liquid measures, measuring spoons, small saucepan, mixing spoon

1.			
Canned crushed pineapple, with juice	3/4 cup	175 mL
Cinnamon honey	2 tbsp.	30 mL
Butter	1 tbsp.	15 mL
Cornstarch	1 tsp.	5 mL

1. Put pineapple with juice into saucepan. Add remaining 3 ingredients. Stir until well mixed. Cook and stir on medium for about 10 minutes until boiling and thickened. Remove pan from heat. Cool. Makes about 1 cup (250 mL)—enough for 2 rockin' kids.

1 serving: 176 Calories; 5.5 g Total Fat (0 g Mono, 0 g Poly, 3.5 g Sat); 15 mg Cholesterol; 31 g Carbohydrate; 1 g Fibre; 0 g Protein; 53 mg Sodium

Pictured on page 68.

Monsieur Auk-Auk Tip: If you don't have cinnamon honey, just use the same amount of regular honey with a sprinkle of ground cinnamon.

Store the leftover crushed pineapple in an airtight container in the refrigerator for up to 1 week.

If you aren't sharing the sauce with a friend, save the other half in an airtight container in the refrigerator for up to 1 week. Reheat the sauce in the microwave, covered, on high (100%) for 30 seconds. Stir. Microwave for another 30 seconds.

1. Don't Box Me In Pudding, page 67
2. Marshmallow Berry Meld, page 70
3. Wonka's Dream Sauce, page 70
4. Rock-A-Hula Sauce, above

Marshmallow Berry Meld

When marshmallow and berries become fused, an unstoppable topping is born! Great over ice cream or cake.

Get It Together: sharp knife, cutting board, measuring spoons, dry measures, small saucepan, mixing spoon

1.	**Large marshmallows, cut up**	3	3
	Milk	2 tbsp.	30 mL
	Butter	1 tbsp.	15 mL
2.	**Frozen mixed berries**	1/2 cup	125 mL
	Icing (confectioner's) sugar	1/4 cup	60 mL

1. Put first 3 ingredients into saucepan. Cook and stir on low for about 5 minutes until marshmallows are melted and hot.

2. Add berries and icing sugar. Cook and stir for 2 to 3 minutes until berries are softened and warm. Makes about 2/3 cup (150 mL)— enough for 1 kid.

1 serving: 322 Calories; 11.7 g Total Fat (trace Mono, trace Poly, 7.4 g Sat); 33 mg Cholesterol; 53 g Carbohydrate; 2 g Fibre; 2 g Protein; 124 mg Sodium

Pictured on page 68.

Wonka's Dream Sauce

A chocolate and caramel sauce that's perfect for pouring on pancakes or dipping with fruit or cookies.

Get It Together: dry measures, measuring spoons, small saucepan, mixing spoon

1.	**Brown sugar, packed**	1/4 cup	60 mL
	Butter	2 tbsp.	30 mL
	Water	1 tbsp.	15 mL
2.	**Whipping cream**	3 tbsp.	50 mL
3.	**Semi-sweet chocolate chips**	2 tbsp.	30 mL

1. Put first 3 ingredients into saucepan. Heat and stir on medium-low for 3 to 5 minutes until sugar is dissolved.

(continued on next page)

Boil It!

2. Add whipping cream. Cook, uncovered, for 10 to 12 minutes, stirring occasionally, until boiling and thickened enough to coat spoon when lifted from mixture. Remove pan from heat.

3. Add chocolate chips. Stir until smooth. Makes about 1/2 cup (125 mL)—enough sauce for 2 chocolate-craving kids.

1 serving: 328 Calories; 22.0 g Total Fat (3.3 g Mono, 0.4 g Poly, 13.7 g Sat); 59 mg Cholesterol; 34 g Carbohydrate; 1 g Fibre; 1 g Protein; 110 mg Sodium

Pictured on page 68.

Oodles Of Noodles Soup

Do you go gaga for noodles? Then, this is your soup!

Get It Together: liquid measures, dry measures, medium saucepan, mixing spoon

1.	Vegetable cocktail juice	1 cup	250 mL
	Water	1 cup	250 mL
2.	Package of instant noodles with seasoning packet	3 oz.	85 g
	Frozen mixed vegetables	1 cup	250 mL

1. Put vegetable cocktail and water into saucepan. Bring to a boil on medium-high.

2. Break noodles into large chunks. Carefully add noodles with seasoning packet and mixed vegetables to juice mixture. Stir. Turn down heat to medium-low. Cook, uncovered, for 3 to 4 minutes, stirring occasionally, until vegetables start to soften. Makes about 3 cups (750 mL)—oodles of soup for 2 kids.

1 serving: 222 Calories; 0.8 g Total Fat (trace Mono, 0.1 g Poly, 0.1 g Sat); 0 mg Cholesterol; 46 g Carbohydrate; 5 g Fibre; 10 g Protein; 818 mg Sodium

Pictured on page 73.

Monsieur Auk-Auk Tip: Use your favourite flavour of instant noodle soup.

Bandito's Broth

Say *olé* to this creamy Mexican-flavoured cheese and chicken soup. Add extra salsa if you're an extreme bandito.

Get It Together: can opener, liquid measures, sharp knife, cutting board, dry measures, grater, small saucepan, mixing spoon, small cup, ladle, 2 soup bowls

1. Canned condensed cream of chicken soup (about half of a 10 oz., 284 mL, can)	1/2 cup	125 mL
Chopped cooked chicken	1/2 cup	125 mL
Chunky salsa	1/2 cup	125 mL
Frozen mixed vegetables	1/2 cup	125 mL
Milk	1/2 cup	125 mL
2. Grated medium Cheddar cheese	1/2 cup	125 mL
Tortilla corn chips, broken into large pieces	1/2 cup	125 mL
3. Tortilla corn chips, broken into large pieces	1/2 cup	125 mL

1. Put first 5 ingredients into saucepan. Mix well. Heat and stir on medium for about 8 minutes until boiling. Turn down heat to medium-low. Cook, uncovered, for another 2 minutes until vegetables are soft.

2. Put 2 tbsp. (30 mL) cheese into cup. Set aside. Add remaining cheese and first amount of chips to soup mixture. Heat and stir for about 30 seconds until cheese is melted and chips are softened. Ladle soup into bowls.

3. Sprinkle half of second amount of tortilla chips and remaining cheese over each bowl of soup. Makes about 2 cups (500 mL)—enough for 2 banditos.

1 serving: 390 Calories; 20.0 g Total Fat (5.0 g Mono, 2.0 g Poly, 8.8 g Sat); 71 mg Cholesterol; 29 g Carbohydrate; 4 g Fibre; 23 g Protein; 1166 mg Sodium

Pictured on page 73.

Monsieur Auk-Auk Tip: Store the remaining condensed soup in an airtight container in the refrigerator for up to 3 days. Use it to make another batch of Bandito's Broth or in another recipe.

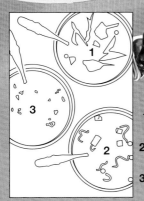

Smashed Potato Soup

Mashed potatoes in a soup? It's simply smashing!

Get It Together: vegetable peeler, sharp knife, cutting board, dry measures, liquid measures, measuring spoons, grater, small saucepan, potato masher, mixing spoon

1. **Chopped peeled potato**	1 cup	250 mL
Water	1/2 cup	125 mL
Chopped onion	1/4 cup	60 mL
2. **Grated mozzarella cheese**	1/2 cup	125 mL
Milk	1/2 cup	125 mL
Parsley flakes	1 tsp.	5 mL
Salt, sprinkle		
Pepper, sprinkle		

1. Put first 3 ingredients into saucepan. Bring to a boil. Turn down heat to medium. Cook, uncovered, for about 10 minutes, stirring occasionally, until potatoes are soft. Remove pan from heat. Mash with potato masher.

2. Add remaining 5 ingredients. Heat and stir on medium-low for about 2 minutes until cheese is melted. Makes about 1 1/2 cups (375 mL)—enough soup for you and a friend.

1 serving: 191 Calories; 7.7 g Total Fat (1.9 g Mono, 0.3 g Poly, 4.6 g Sat); 28 mg Cholesterol; 22 g Carbohydrate; 2 g Fibre; 9 g Protein; 146 mg Sodium

Pictured on page 73.

Ham & Pea Hide-&-Seek

Ham and peas play hide-and-seek in cheesy pasta shells.

Get It Together: liquid measures, measuring spoons, dry measures, sharp knife, cutting board, large saucepan, mixing spoon, strainer

1. **Water**	4 cups	1 L
Salt	1/2 tsp.	2 mL
Small shell pasta	1 cup	250 mL
Frozen peas	1 cup	250 mL
2. **Finely chopped ham**	1 1/4 cups	300 mL
Process cheese spread	1/2 cup	125 mL

(continued on next page)

Boil It!

1. Put water and salt into saucepan. Bring to a boil on medium-high. Add pasta. Cook, uncovered, for 8 minutes, stirring occasionally. Add peas. Cook, uncovered, for about 3 minutes, stirring occasionally, until pasta is soft. Use strainer to drain pasta mixture. Return pasta mixture to same pot.

2. Add ham and cheese spread. Turn heat down to medium-low. Heat and stir for about 1 minute until pasta is coated and ham is warm. Makes about 3 1/2 cups (875 mL)—enough for you to share with a friend because playing hide-and-seek alone is no fun.

1 serving: *588 Calories; 22.8 g Total Fat (3.9 g Mono, 1.1 g Poly, 11.6 g Sat); 129 mg Cholesterol; 51 g Carbohydrate; 5 g Fibre; 43 g Protein; 1218 mg Sodium*

Pictured below.

Left: Neptune's Num-Nums, page 76 Right: Ham & Pea Hide-&-Seek, page 74

Neptune's Num-Nums

Tuna and cheesy pasta shells make a snack fit for a king, or queen, of the sea!

Get It Together: liquid measures, dry measures, sharp knife, cutting board, measuring spoons, large saucepan with lid, mixing spoon, strainer

1.	**Water**	4 cups	1 L
	Salt	1/2 tsp.	2 mL
	Small shell pasta	1 cup	250 mL
	Finely chopped celery	1/4 cup	60 mL
2.	**Frozen peas**	1/4 cup	60 mL
3.	**Herb and garlic cream cheese**	1/4 cup	60 mL
	Milk	2 tbsp.	30 mL
	Can of chunk light tuna in water, drained	6 oz.	170 g
4.	**Process cheese slices**	2	2

1. Put water and salt into saucepan. Bring to a boil on medium-high. Add pasta and celery. Cook, uncovered, for 7 minutes, stirring occasionally.

2. Add peas. Cook for about 1 minute, stirring occasionally, until pasta is soft. Use strainer to drain pasta mixture. Return pasta mixture to same pan.

3. Add cream cheese and milk. Cook and stir on medium for about 2 minutes until cream cheese is melted. Add tuna. Stir gently. Turn down heat to medium-low.

4. Place cheese slices over tuna mixture. Cover with lid. Cook for 2 minutes. Heat and stir for about 1 minute until tuna mixture is hot and cheese slices are melted. Be careful not to let the cheese burn. Makes about 2 cups (500 mL)—a good amount for 2 kids to share.

1 serving: 465 Calories; 17.3 g Total Fat (0.2 g Mono, 0.6 g Poly, 10.5 g Sat); 72 mg Cholesterol; 41 g Carbohydrate; 3 g Fibre; 34 g Protein; 525 mg Sodium

Pictured on page 75.

Q: Where does a man-eating fish hang out?

A: At a seafood restaurant.

Abracadabra Omelette

Amaze your friends with your magical skills. All you need is a freezer bag and, abracadabra, a perfect omelette appears!

Get It Together: sharp knife, cutting board, grater, measuring spoons, liquid measures, small resealable freezer bag, medium saucepan, tongs, plate

1.			
Large eggs		2	2
Diced ham		2 tbsp.	30 mL
Grated medium Cheddar cheese		2 tbsp.	30 mL
2. Water		5 cups	1.25 L

1. Put first 3 ingredients into freezer bag. Seal bag. Squeeze, squish and shake ingredients in bag until well mixed.

2. Put water into saucepan. Bring to a boil. Turn down heat to medium-low. Place freezer bag in water. Cook, uncovered, for 12 to 14 minutes until egg is firm. Remove bag from water with tongs. Let cool for 1 minute. Carefully open bag. Slide omelette onto plate. Makes 1 perfect omelette.

1 serving: 233 Calories; 15.3 g Total Fat (2.1 g Mono, 0.3 g Poly, 6.5 g Sat); 461 mg Cholesterol; 2 g Carbohydrate; 0 g Fibre; 20.5 g Protein; 228 mg Sodium

Pictured below.

Monsieur Auk-Auk Tip:
Make sure you use a freezer bag and not a sandwich bag because it's stronger for cooking.

Abracadabra Omelette, above

Bake It!

Here's where you get to use the oven. Remember—oven mitts are mandatory!

Q1: Say toast 10 times quickly. What do you put in a toaster?

Q2: What do you get when you cross a chili pepper, a shovel and a golden retriever?

Q3: What is a full turkey called?

Chillin' Cheese Toast

Chili out! The coolest way to eat chili is on a cheesy slice of toast.

Get It Together: measuring spoons, can opener, grater, baking sheet with sides, table knife, spoon, oven mitts, wire rack

1.			
Texas bread slice	1	1
Spreadable cream cheese	1 tbsp.	15 mL
Canned chili	2 tbsp.	30 mL
Grated medium Cheddar cheese	2 tbsp.	30 mL

1. Place oven rack in centre position. Turn oven on to 375°F (190°C). Place bread slice on baking sheet. Gently spread cream cheese on bread slice. Spoon chili onto centre of bread slice. Sprinkle with cheese. Bake for about 15 minutes until bread is lightly browned. Put baking sheet on wire rack to cool. Let cool for 2 minutes. Turn oven off. Makes 1 tasty toast.

1 serving: 213 Calories; 7.8 g Total Fat (0 g Mono, 0 g Poly, 5.1 g Sat); 21 mg Cholesterol; 26 g Carbohydrate; 2 g Fibre; 9 g Protein; 509 mg Sodium

Pictured below.

Creampuff Tip: Leftover chili can be served on hot dogs or hamburgers to make chili dogs or chili burgers. You can also put it on French fries to make chili fries. If you're not using the leftover chili in the next day or 2, store it in an airtight container in the freezer.

Chillin' Cheese Toast, above

Big Daddy Garlic Toast

Make garlic cheese toast just like they do in restaurants.

Get It Together: measuring spoons, sharp knife, cutting board, grater, foil, baking sheet with sides, table knife, oven mitts, wire rack

1.	**Butter**	**1 tsp.**	**5 mL**
	Bread slice, toasted	**1**	**1**
	Garlic clove, cut in half	**1**	**1**
2.	**Grated mozzarella cheese**	**2 tbsp.**	**30 mL**

1. Place oven rack in centre position. Turn oven broiler on. Line baking sheet with foil. Spread butter on bread slice. Rub bread slice lightly with cut side of garlic. Discard garlic. Place bread, butter-side up, on baking sheet.

2. Sprinkle with cheese. Broil for about 3 minutes until cheese is melted and starting to brown. Put baking sheet on wire rack to cool. Let cool for 2 minutes. Turn broiler off. Makes 1 toast for 1 lucky kid.

1 serving: 145 Calories; 8.5 g Total Fat (2.0 g Mono, 0.3 g Poly, 4.3 g Sat); 22 mg Cholesterol; 13 g Carbohydrate; 0 g Fibre; 5 g Protein; 217 mg Sodium

Pictured on page 81.

Creampuff Tip: You don't have to peel the garlic clove. Just cut it in half.

Ragin' Cajun Wedges

A little spice is always nice! Serve with ranch dressing or salsa and sour cream for dipping.

Get It Together: measuring spoons, grater, dry measures, baking sheet with sides, foil, cooking spray, fork, paper towel, oven mitts, sharp knife, cutting board, wire rack

1.	**Large potato**	**1**	**1**
2.	**Grated jalapeño Monterey Jack cheese**	**1/2 cup**	**125 mL**
	Cajun seasoning	**1/2 tsp.**	**2 mL**

(continued on next page)

1. Put oven rack in centre position. Turn oven on to 425°F (220°C). Line baking sheet with foil. Grease foil with cooking spray. Set aside. Poke potato all over with fork. Wrap potato in paper towel. Microwave on high (100%) for 3 minutes. Use oven mitts to turn potato over. Microwave for another 3 minutes. The potato is cooked when you can easily poke it with a fork. Let potato stand for about 5 minutes until cool enough to handle. Cut potato from end to end into 8 long wedges. Spray each wedge with cooking spray. Place wedges side by side and close together on baking sheet.

2. Sprinkle cheese and seasoning over wedges. Bake for about 10 minutes until cheese is melted and wedges are hot. Place baking sheet on wire rack to cool. Let cool for 5 minutes. Turn oven off. Makes enough wedges for 2 kids to share.

1 serving: *241 Calories; 9.2 g Total Fat (0 g Mono, 0.1 g Poly, 5.0 g Sat); 25 mg Cholesterol; 33 g Carbohydrate; 3 g Fibre; 9 g Protein; 335 mg Sodium*

Pictured below.

Left: Big Daddy Garlic Toast, page 80   Right: Ragin' Cajun Wedges, page 80

Nicely Spicy Crisps

Are you nice enough to share these golden-brown potato moons?

Get It Together: measuring spoons, foil, baking sheet with sides, cooking spray, sharp knife, cutting board, medium bowl, mixing spoons, oven mitts, wire rack

1. **Large potato** — 1 — 1
   Cooking oil — 1 tsp. — 5 mL

2. **Grated Parmesan cheese** — 1 tbsp. — 15 mL
   Chili powder — 1/8 tsp. — 0.5 mL
   Seasoned salt — 1/8 tsp. — 0.5 mL

1. Place oven rack in centre position. Turn oven on to 450°F (230°C). Line baking sheet with foil. Grease foil with cooking spray. Set aside. Cut potato in half from end to end. Cut potato halves from side to side into 1/4 inch (6 mm) thick slices. Put potato slices into bowl. Drizzle with cooking oil.

2. Sprinkle next 3 ingredients over potato slices. Use mixing spoons to toss until coated. Arrange potato slices in a single layer on baking sheet. Spray tops of potato slices with cooking spray. Bake for 15 minutes. Turn potato slices over. Bake for another 15 minutes until browned. Put baking sheet on wire rack to cool. Let cool for 5 minutes. Turn oven off. Makes plenty of crisps for 2 hungry kids.

1 serving: 175 Calories; 3.7 g Total Fat (1.5 g Mono, 0.8 g Poly, 1.0 g Sat); 4 mg Cholesterol; 32 g Carbohydrate; 3 g Fibre; 5 g Protein; 130 mg Sodium

Pictured on page 84.

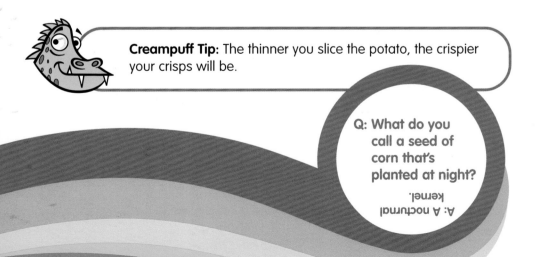

Creampuff Tip: The thinner you slice the potato, the crispier your crisps will be.

Q: What do you call a seed of corn that's planted at night?

A: A nocturnal kernel.

Big Tex's Beef Dippers

For whenever you're a-hankerin' for some big ranch BBQ taste.

Get It Together: measuring spoons, liquid measures, table knife, foil, oven mitts, wire rack, small bowl, mixing spoon

1.	English muffins, split	2	2
	Butter	2 tsp.	10 mL
2.	Prepared mustard	1/2 tsp.	2 mL
	Garlic powder	1/4 tsp.	1 mL
3.	Deli shaved roast beef	4 oz.	113 g
4.	Barbecue sauce	1/4 cup	60 mL
	Prepared beef broth	1/4 cup	60 mL

1. Place oven rack in centre position. Turn oven on to 400°F (205°C). Toast muffin halves until brown and crispy. Spread 1/2 tsp. (2 mL) butter on each muffin half.

2. Spread 1/4 tsp. (1 mL) mustard on 1 half of each muffin. Sprinkle garlic powder on other muffin halves.

3. Place half of roast beef over mustard on each muffin. Place other muffin halves over roast beef, garlic powder-side down. Cut two 9 x 12 inch (22 x 30 cm) pieces of foil. Wrap 1 muffin in each piece of foil. Bake for 10 to 12 minutes until hot. Put foil-wrapped muffins on wire rack to cool. Turn oven off.

4. Put barbecue sauce and broth into bowl. Mix well. Carefully remove foil from muffins. Serve muffins with sauce mixture for dipping. Makes 2 dippers for 2 hungry kids.

1 serving: 241 Calories; 3.0 g Total Fat (0.1 g Mono, 0.1 g Poly, 3.0 g Sat); 42 mg Cholesterol; 29 g Carbohydrate; 2 g Fibre; 16 g Protein; 989 mg Sodium

Pictured on page 84.

Q: What did the cook give his girlfriend?

A: A 14-carrot onion ring.

Fully-Loaded Potato Puffs

Loaded up with baked potato fixin's,
these tasty tots are sure to rev up your engine.

Get It Together: measuring spoons, sharp knife, cutting board, 9 inch (22 cm) pie plate, cooking spray, oven mitts, wire rack, spoon

1.	Frozen potato tots (gems or puffs)	16	16
2.	Process Cheddar cheese slices	2	2
	Bacon bits	1 tbsp.	15 mL
	Chopped green onion	1 tbsp.	15 mL
3.	Sour cream	1 tbsp.	15 mL

1. Put oven rack in centre position. Turn oven on to 450°F (230°C). Grease pie plate with cooking spray. Arrange potato tots in pie plate. Bake for 10 to 12 minutes until golden.

2. Cut or tear cheese slices into small pieces. Sprinkle over potato tots. Sprinkle with bacon bits and green onion. Bake for another 3 to 5 minutes until cheese is melted. Put pie plate on wire rack to cool. Turn oven off. Let cool for 5 minutes. Turn oven off.

3. Spoon sour cream on top. Makes enough to share with a friend.

1 serving: 221 Calories; 11.7 g Total Fat (2.6 g Mono, 0.1 g Poly, 5.0 g Sat); 23 mg Cholesterol; 21 g Carbohydrate; 2 g Fibre; 7 g Protein; 722 mg Sodium

Pictured on page 84.

Creampuff Tip: You can sprinkle 1/4 cup (60 mL) grated Mexican cheese blend over the potato tots instead of using the cheese slices.

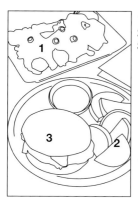

1. Fully-Loaded Potato Puffs, above
2. Nicely Spicy Crisps, page 82
3. Big Tex's Beef Dippers, page 83

NYU Pizza

Not Your Usual Pizza. Combines 2 all-time
favourite snacks in 1—pizza and chips!

Get It Together: measuring spoons, grater, dry measures, baking sheet
with sides, cooking spray, spoon, oven mitts, wire rack, cutting board,
sharp knife

1.	**Flour tortilla (9 inch, 22 cm, diameter)**	1	1
	Pizza sauce	1 tbsp.	15 mL
2.	**Grated mozzarella cheese**	1/4 cup	60 mL
	Coarsely crushed potato chips	1/4 cup	60 mL

1. Place oven rack in centre position. Turn oven on to 375°F (190°C).
   Grease baking sheet with cooking spray. Place tortilla on baking sheet.
   Spread pizza sauce on top, leaving about 1/2 inch (12 mm) edge.

2. Sprinkle 2 tbsp. (30 mL) cheese over sauce. Sprinkle with chips.
   Sprinkle remaining cheese over top. Bake for about 10 minutes
   until cheese is bubbling and golden. Put baking sheet on wire rack to
   cool. Let cool for 2 minutes. Turn oven off. Carefully slide pizza onto
   cutting board. Cut into 4 wedges. Makes 1 unusual pizza.

1 serving: 293 Calories; 15.3 g Total Fat (1.0 g Mono, 2.6 g Poly, 6.0 g Sat); 15 mg Cholesterol;
31 g Carbohydrate; 1 g Fibre; 12 g Protein; 635 mg Sodium

Pictured on page 87.

Creampuff Tip: Use your favourite flavour of potato chips—or
mix up a bunch of flavours, if you dare! Try using grated
mozzarella and Cheddar cheese blend with BBQ chips or use
grated mozzarella cheese with salt and vinegar chips.

**Q: Why didn't
the chicken cross
the road?**

A: He was chicken.

Left: Sandwich Alfredo, below Right: NYU Pizza, page 86

Sandwich Alfredo

Who needs pasta to enjoy alfredo sauce?
Mama mia, it's just as good in a sandwich!

Get It Together: measuring spoons, sharp knife, cutting board, dry measures, grater, baking sheet with sides, cooking spray, table knife, oven mitts, wire rack

1.			
Texas bread slices, toasted	2	2
Alfredo pasta sauce	2 tbsp.	30 mL
Chopped ham	1/4 cup	60 mL
Grated mozzarella cheese	1/4 cup	60 mL

1. Place oven rack in top position. Turn oven broiler on. Grease baking sheet with cooking spray. Place bread slices on baking sheet.
    Spread 1 tbsp. (15 mL) alfredo sauce on each bread slice. Sprinkle ham over sauce on 1 bread slice. Sprinkle cheese over sauce on other bread slice. Broil for about 5 minutes until cheese is melted and bubbly.
    Put baking sheet on wire rack to cool. Let cool for 1 minute. Turn broiler off. Place cheese-topped slice over ham-topped slice, cheese-side down. Cut sandwich in half. Makes 1 really tasty sandwich.

1 serving: 429 Calories; 17.5 g Total Fat (3.4 g Mono, 0.5 g Poly, 8.7 g Sat); 67 mg Cholesterol; 44 g Carbohydrate; 2 g Fibre; 22 g Protein; 721 mg Sodium

Pictured above.

Dog 'N' Bean Cups

Wieners and beans are downright purty dressed up in their own bread cups.

Get It Together: sharp knife, cutting board, can opener, measuring spoons, grater, 2 ramekins, baking sheet with sides, oven mitts, wire rack, small bowl, mixing spoon

1. **Bread slices** — 2 — 2

2. **Wiener, chopped** — 1 — 1
   Canned baked beans in tomato sauce — 2 tbsp. — 30 mL
   Salsa — 1 tbsp. — 15 mL
   Grated mozzarella cheese — 2 tbsp. — 30 mL

1. Place oven rack in centre position. Turn oven on to 350°F (175°C). Cut crusts off bread slices. Press bread slices into bottom and sides of ramekins. It's okay if the corners stick out. Place ramekins on baking sheet. Bake for 10 to 12 minutes until lightly browned. Put baking sheet on wire rack. Turn down heat in oven to 325°F (160°C).

2. Put next 3 ingredients into bowl. Mix well. Spoon wiener mixture into toast cups. Sprinkle cheese over top. Bake for about 15 minutes until hot. Put baking sheet on wire rack to cool. Let cool for 5 minutes. Turn oven off. Makes 2 super snacks.

1 serving: 162 Calories; 7.5 g Total Fat (2.1 g Mono, 0.4 g Poly, 2.5 g Sat); 13 mg Cholesterol; 18 g Carbohydrate; 1 g Fibre; 7 g Protein; 485 mg Sodium

Pictured on page 89

Creampuff Tip: Leftover baked beans can be stored in an airtight container in the freezer or added to a chili, soup or stew.

Q: Why did the elephant eat a candle?

A: He wanted a light snack.

Top: Dog 'N' Bean Cups, above Bottom: Blackbeard's Treasure Chests, page 90

Bake It!

Blackbeard's Treasure Chests

If you're not afraid of the pirate's curse, you're bound
to find a golden filling in these treasure chests.

Get It Together: sharp knife, cutting board, dry measures, measuring
spoons, small bowl, mixing spoon, small cup, fork, baking sheet with sides,
pastry brush, spoon, oven mitts, wire rack

1.			
	Chopped cooked chicken	1/2 cup	125 mL
	Plain yogurt	2 tbsp.	30 mL
	Raisins	2 tbsp.	30 mL
	Curry powder	1/2 tsp.	2 mL
	Salt	1/4 tsp.	1 mL
	Pepper	1/8 tsp.	0.5 mL
2.	Large egg	1	1
	Water	1 tbsp.	15 mL
3.	Unbaked tart shells	8	8

1. Place oven rack in centre position. Turn oven on to 400°F (190°C).
   Put first 6 ingredients into bowl. Mix well. Set aside.

2. Break egg into cup. Add water. Beat egg a little with fork.

3. Place 4 tart shells on baking sheet. Spoon 2 tbsp. (30 mL) chicken
   mixture into each tart shell. Brush edges of filled tarts with egg mixture
   using pastry brush. Carefully remove 1 of the remaining tart shells from
   foil liner. Gently place shell, upside-down, over top of a filled tart.
   Press edges gently to seal. Repeat with remaining tart shells.
   Use remaining egg mixture to brush tops of tarts. Bake for about
   15 minutes until golden. Put baking sheet on wire rack to cool.
   Let cool for 5 minutes. Turn oven off. Makes 4 treasure-filled chests
   for 2 brave kids.

1 serving: 487 Calories; 26.3 g Total Fat (10.0 g Mono, 8.7 g Poly, 4.7 g Sat); 139 mg Cholesterol;
43 g Carbohydrate; 1 g Fibre; 18 g Protein; 801 mg Sodium

Pictured on page 89.

According to the
Guinness World
Records, the
largest sandwich
weighed 5,440
lbs. (2,467.5 kg)!

Bake It!

Tutti-Frutti Mini-Crisps

These crispy fruit cups are fruit-errific!

Get It Together: dry measures, measuring spoons, sharp knife, can opener, cutting board, 2 ramekins, cooking spray, baking sheet with sides, 2 small bowls, mixing spoon, oven mitts, wire rack

1.	Quick-cooking rolled oats	1/2 cup	125 mL
	Butter, melted	1/4 cup	60 mL
	All-purpose flour	2 tbsp.	30 mL
	Brown sugar, packed	2 tbsp.	30 mL
	Ground cinnamon	1/8 tsp.	0.5 mL
2.	Canned pineapple tidbits, drained	1/2 cup	125 mL
	Diced banana	1/2 cup	125 mL
	Lemon juice	2 tsp.	10 mL

1. Place oven rack in centre position. Turn oven on to 350°F (175°C). Grease ramekins with cooking spray. Place ramekins on baking sheet. Set aside. Put first 5 ingredients into 1 bowl. Stir until mixture resembles coarse crumbs.

2. Put next 3 ingredients into other bowl. Stir. Spoon fruit mixture into ramekins. Sprinkle oat mixture over top. Bake for about 30 minutes until golden. Put baking sheet on wire rack to cool. Let cool for 5 minutes. Turn oven off. Makes 2 terrific treats.

1 serving: 425 Calories; 23.7 g Total Fat (trace Mono, trace Poly, 14.0 g Sat); 60 mg Cholesterol; 50 g Carbohydrate; 4 g Fibre; 4 g Protein; 192 mg Sodium

Pictured on page 92.

Creampuff Tip: To melt butter, measure into small microwave-safe dish. Microwave on high (100%) for 10 seconds. Stir until melted.

Q: What are the 3 flavours in Neapolitan ice cream?

A: Chocolate, strawberry, vanilla.

Top: Tutti-Frutti Mini-Crisps, page 91 Bottom: Cinnamon Hypnotizers, below

Cinnamon Hypnotizers

Stare too long and you'll be hypnotized by these whirly twirly cinnamon pinwheels.

Get It Together: measuring spoons, baking sheet with sides, cooking spray, small bowl, mixing spoon, pastry brush, oven mitts, wire rack, sharp knife, cutting board

1.	Brown sugar, packed	3 tbsp.	50 mL
	Ground cinnamon	1 tsp.	5 mL
2.	Flour tortillas (9 inch, 22 cm, diameter)	2	2
	Butter, melted	3 tbsp.	50 mL

1. Place oven rack in centre position. Turn oven on to 350°F (175°C). Grease baking sheet with cooking spray. Set aside. Put brown sugar and cinnamon into bowl. Mix well.

2. Brush tortillas with half of butter using pastry brush. Sprinkle half of brown sugar mixture on each tortilla. Roll tortillas up tightly, jelly roll-style. Place rolls, seam-side down, on baking sheet. Brush with remaining butter. Bake for 8 to 10 minutes until rolls are golden. Put baking sheet on wire rack to cool. Let cool for 5 minutes. Turn oven off. Cut rolls into 1/2 inch (12 mm) thick slices. Makes about 28 hypnotizers—enough to get you and a friend really dizzy.

1 serving: 332 Calories; 19.0 g Total Fat (0 g Mono, 0 g Poly, 11.0 g Sat); 45 mg Cholesterol; 37 g Carbohydrate; 1 g Fibre; 2 g Protein; 368 mg Sodium

Pictured above.

Plan It!

We know. You're a busy person. If you prefer to grab your snack and go, this is the chapter for you. Here you whip up a bunch of snacks that you can save to eat whenever you want. And no matter your skill level—there's a big-batch recipe you can make in this section.

Personal food profile

My name is: _____

My favourite vegetable is: _____

My favourite fruit is: _____

My favourite meat is: _____

My favourite dessert is: _____

My favourite drink is: _____

My favourite meal is: _____

My least favourite meal is: _____

I would never eat: _____

If I had a restaurant, I would name it: _____

In my restaurant I would serve: _____

Food trivia

Did you know that a tomato is actually a fruit? Fruits have seeds inside them and vegetables don't!

Do you know that pepper was once the most expensive spice in the world?

Did you know that French fries were actually invented in Belgium? And Belgians often serve their fries with mayonnaise!

Señor Piquante Chili Bites

Yow! These babies have a spicy, fiery bite. Are you brave enough to try?

Get It Together: liquid measures, grater, dry measures, measuring spoons, mini-muffin pan, cooking spray, small bowl, fork, spoon, wooden toothpick, oven mitts, wire rack, table knife, plate

1.			
Large eggs	2	2	
Grated jalapeño Monterey Jack cheese	1/2 cup	125 mL	
Chunky salsa	1/4 cup	60 mL	
Crushed Ritz crackers (about 8 crackers)	1/4 cup	60 mL	
Chili powder	1/2 tsp.	2 mL	

1. Place oven rack in centre position. Turn oven on to 425°F (220°C). Grease muffin cups with cooking spray. Break eggs into bowl. Beat eggs a little with fork. Add remaining 4 ingredients. Mix well. Spoon about 1 1/2 tbsp. (25 mL) cheese mixture into each muffin cup. Bake for 8 to 10 minutes until toothpick inserted straight down into centre of a bite comes out clean. Put pan on wire rack. Turn oven off. Let cool for 2 minutes. Run knife around inside edge of muffin cups to loosen bites. Transfer to plate. Makes 12 bites.

1 bite: 54 Calories; 3.4 g Total Fat (1.2 g Mono, 0.2 g Poly, 1.3 g Sat); 35 mg Cholesterol; 4 g Carbohydrate; trace Fibre; 2 g Protein; 115 mg Sodium

Pictured on page 96.

Monsieur Auk-Auk Tip: Store bites in resealable sandwich bags in sets of 3 in the refrigerator for up to 5 days. Eat cold or reheat in the microwave on high (100%) for about 15 seconds until hot.

Q: What is a cannibal's favourite game?

A: Swallow the leader.

Surf's Up Pizza Pandemonium

There's enough mini-Hawaiian pizzas here to keep you hangin' ten for over a week!

Get It Together: liquid measures, sharp knife, cutting board, dry measures, can opener, grater, baking sheet with sides, cooking spray, spoon, strainer, oven mitts, wire rack

1.	**Tube of refrigerator pizza dough**	10 oz.	283 g
2.	**Pizza sauce**	1/2 cup	125 mL
	Chopped ham	3/4 cup	175 mL
3.	**Canned crushed pineapple, drained**	1/2 cup	125 mL
	Grated mozzarella cheese	1 cup	250 mL

1. Place oven rack in centre position. Turn oven on to 400°F (205°C). Remove pizza dough from wrapping but do not unroll. Slice pizza dough roll into eight 1 inch (2.5 cm) slices. Press each slice out to 3 1/2 inch (9 cm) wide circle, about 1/8 inch (3 mm) thick. Grease baking sheet with cooking spray. Arrange circles in a single layer on baking sheet.

2. Spread 1 tbsp. (15 mL) sauce on each circle. Sprinkle ham over sauce.

3. Press pineapple in strainer until no more liquid comes out. Spread pineapple over ham. Sprinkle cheese over top. Bake for about 20 minutes until golden. Put baking sheet on wire rack. Turn oven off. Let cool for 5 minutes. Makes 8 mini-pizzas.

1 mini-pizza: 175 Calories; 6.1 g Total Fat (1.5 g Mono, 0.2 g Poly, 2.4 g Sat); 23 mg Cholesterol; 20 g Carbohydrate; 1 g Fibre; 10 g Protein; 327 mg Sodium

Pictured on page 96.

Monsieur Auk-Auk Tip: Leftover crushed pineapple may be stored in an airtight container in the refrigerator for up to 3 days.

Store your pizzas in an airtight container in the freezer for up to 1 month. To reheat, place a frozen pizza on a paper towel-lined plate. Microwave on high (100%) for about 60 seconds until hot.

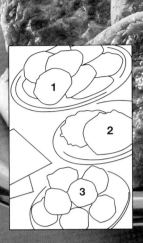

Presto Pizzeria Buns

Just say "Presto," and you'll change-o these regular rolls into pizza buns.

Get It Together: grater, dry measures, measuring spoons, baking sheet with sides, cooking spray, waxed paper, tea towel, small bowl, mixing spoon, oven mitts, wire rack

1. **Package of frozen unbaked dinner rolls, covered, thawed in refrigerator overnight**	1 lb.	454 g
2. **Grated mild Cheddar cheese**	1/3 cup	75 mL
Grated Parmesan cheese	1/3 cup	75 mL
Pizza sauce	1/4 cup	60 mL

1. Grease baking sheet with cooking spray. Place rolls on baking sheet in 3 rows, 4 across. Press each roll into a 3 1/2 inch (9 cm) wide circle. It's okay if rolls are touching one another. Grease waxed paper with cooking spray. Cover rolls with waxed paper, greased-side down. Place tea towel over top. Let sit in oven with light on and door closed for 30 minutes. Remove baking sheet from oven.

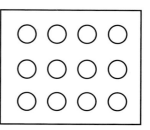

2. Place oven rack in centre position. Turn oven on to 375°F (190°C). Put Cheddar and Parmesan cheese into bowl. Mix well. Spread 1 tsp. (5 mL) pizza sauce on each bun, leaving 1/2 inch (12 mm) border. Sprinkle 1 tbsp. (15 mL) cheese mixture over pizza sauce. Bake for about 18 minutes until lightly browned. Put baking sheet on wire rack. Turn oven off. Let cool for 5 minutes. Makes 12 pizza buns.

1 bun: 180 Calories; 7.0 g Total Fat (1.3 g Mono, 0.1 g Poly, 3.2 g Sat); 13 mg Cholesterol; 18 g Carbohydrate; 1 g Fibre; 10 g Protein; 548 mg Sodium

Pictured on page 96.

Monsieur Auk-Auk Tip: Store the pizza buns in an airtight container or covered with plastic wrap in the refrigerator for up to 3 days. Store in the freezer for up to 1 month. To reheat, microwave on high (100%) for about 30 seconds.

Samurai Sushi Rolls

Grasshopper, do you have what it takes to tackle sushi?
Actually, it's easier to make this simply super sushi than you may think.

Get It Together: dry measures, liquid measures, measuring spoons, sharp knife, cutting board, can opener, strainer, medium saucepan with a lid, mixing spoons, small bowl, waxed paper, fork, plastic wrap

1.	Short grain white rice	1 cup	250 mL
	Water	1 1/2 cups	375 mL
	Salt	1/8 tsp.	0.5 mL
2.	Rice vinegar	2 tbsp.	30 mL
	Granulated sugar	1 tbsp.	15 mL
3.	Cooked chicken, cut into thin strips	1/3 cup	75 mL
	Thick teriyaki basting sauce	2 tbsp.	30 mL
4.	Nori (roasted seaweed) sheets	2	2
5.	Thin strips of red pepper	10	10
6.	Canned pineapple slices, each cut into 4 pieces	2	2

1. Put rice into strainer. Rinse rice under cold water until water runs clear (is no longer cloudy). Put rice into saucepan. Add water and salt. Stir. Bring to a boil. Turn down heat to medium-low. Cover with lid. Cook for about 20 minutes, without lifting lid, until rice is tender. Remove pan from heat. Wait for about 5 minutes until liquid is soaked up.

2. Add rice vinegar and sugar. Mix well. Cool.

3. Put chicken into bowl. Drizzle with teriyaki sauce. Use mixing spoons to toss until coated.

4. Place 1 sheet of nori, shiny-side down, on a sheet of waxed paper with 1 long edge closest to you. Spoon half of rice mixture onto centre of nori. Run fork under water so that it is wet. Spread rice mixture almost to edge of nori using fork, leaving a 2 inch (5 cm) edge on the side farthest from you (see Step A). Lay half of chicken strips across the rice, about 2 inches (5 cm) away from the edge closest to you.

5. Lay half of red pepper slices alongside chicken.

(continued on next page)

Plan It!

6. Lay 4 pieces of pineapple alongside red pepper (see Step B). Dampen 1/2 inch (12 mm) border along edge farthest from you with water. Starting at edge closest to you, roll up tightly, using waxed paper as a guide (see Step C). Repeat with remaining ingredients to make another sushi roll. Cover rolls with plastic wrap. Chill for about 1 hour until cold. Cut each roll into 8 slices (see Step D). Makes 16 slices.

1 slice: 61 Calories; 0.3 g Total Fat (0.1 g Mono, 0.1 g Poly, 0.1 g Sat); 3 mg Cholesterol; 12 g Carbohydrate; trace Fibre; 2 g Protein; 111 mg Sodium

Pictured below.

Monsieur Auk-Auk Tip: Have any leftover chicken strips? They'll work fine in this recipe! If you don't have any leftover, maybe ask a grown-up to cook a couple extra strips for you.

Step A   **Step B**

Step C   **Step D**

Bird's Nest Pies

Make your very own chicken pot pies with a golden biscuit top.

Get It Together: dry measures, sharp knife, cutting board, can opener, baking sheet with sides, foil, four 5 inch (12.5 cm) foil pie plates, medium bowl, mixing spoon, small bowl, whisk, pastry brush, oven mitts, wire rack

1.	Crushed soda crackers (about 8 crackers)	1/3 cup	75 mL
2.	Frozen mixed vegetables, thawed	3 cups	750 mL
	Chopped cooked chicken	1 1/2 cups	375 mL
	Can of condensed cream of chicken soup	10 oz.	284 mL
3.	Tube of refrigerator crescent rolls (8 rolls per tube)	8 1/2 oz.	235 g
4.	Large egg	1	1

1. Place oven rack in centre position. Turn oven on to 350°F (175°C). Line baking sheet with foil. Arrange pie plates on baking sheet. Sprinkle cracker crumbs into pie plates.

2. Put next 3 ingredients into medium bowl. Stir. Spoon into pie plates.

3. Unroll dough. Separate into 8 triangles. Lay 2 triangles on a lightly floured surface, with longest edges slightly overlapping. Press together to make a 5 1/4 inch (13 cm) square. Trim corners to make a round shape. Discard trimmings. Repeat with remaining triangles.

4. Break egg into small bowl. Beat with whisk until bubbly on top. Place circles over pie plates. Press edges of dough against sides of pie plates to seal. Brush dough with egg using pastry brush. Cut three 1 inch (2.5 cm) slits in top of each pie to allow steam to escape during baking. Bake for 25 to 30 minutes until tops are golden and filling is hot. Put baking sheet on wire rack. Turn oven off. Let cool for 5 minutes. Makes 4 chicken pies.

1 pie: 513 Calories; 23.1 g Total Fat (4.1 g Mono, 2.2 g Poly, 6.0 g Sat); 99 mg Cholesterol; 53 g Carbohydrate; 6 g Fibre; 26 g Protein; 589 mg Sodium

Pictured on page 101.

(continued on next page)

Plan It!

Monsieur Auk-Auk Tip: Store the baked pies in an airtight container in the refrigerator for up to 2 days or in the freezer for up to 1 month. To thaw, place in the refrigerator overnight. To reheat, bake in 350°F (175°C) oven for about 25 minutes until filling is hot.

Make sure to be careful when breaking the crust. The steam coming from the pie will be hot!

Bird's Nest Pies, page 100

Gold Rush Muffins

Strike it rich with these muffins full of golden apple nuggets.

Get It Together: dry measures, measuring spoons, liquid measures, sharp knife, cutting board, muffin pan, cooking spray, medium bowl, mixing spoon, small bowl, fork, wooden toothpick, oven mitts, wire rack

1.			
	All-purpose flour	2 cups	500 mL
	Brown sugar, packed	1/2 cup	125 mL
	Baking powder	1 1/2 tsp.	7 mL
	Baking soda	1/2 tsp.	2 mL
	Salt	1/2 tsp.	2 mL
2.	Large egg	1	1
	Vanilla yogurt	1 cup	250 mL
	Syrup	1/4 cup	60 mL
	Applesauce	2 tbsp.	30 mL
	Cooking oil	2 tbsp.	30 mL
3.	Chopped peeled apple	1 cup	250 mL
	Chopped pecans	1/2 cup	125 mL

1. Place oven rack in centre position. Turn oven on to 375°F (190°C). Grease muffin cups with cooking spray. Set aside. Put first 5 ingredients into medium bowl. Stir well. Dig a hole in centre of flour mixture with mixing spoon. Set aside.

2. Break egg into small bowl. Beat egg a little with fork. Add next 4 ingredients. Stir until well mixed. Pour into hole in flour mixture.

3. Add apple and pecans. Stir just until flour mixture is moistened. Fill muffin cups 3/4 full with batter. Bake for 18 to 20 minutes until toothpick inserted straight down into centre of a muffin comes out clean. Put pan on wire rack. Turn oven off. Let cool for 5 minutes. Transfer muffins from pan to wire rack to cool. Makes 12 muffins.

1 muffin: 206 Calories; 6.4 g Total Fat (3.5 g Mono, 1.8 g Poly, 0.7 g Sat); 17 mg Cholesterol; 35 g Carbohydrate; 1 g Fibre; 4 g Protein; 203 mg Sodium

Pictured on page 105.

Monsieur Auk-Auk Tip: Store the muffins in an airtight container or wrapped individually in plastic wrap in the freezer for up to 1 month.

Plan It!

Fanana Of Banana Muffins

Try saying that 5 times fast! If you're a fan of banana and chocolate, these muffins are for you.

Get It Together: dry measures, measuring spoons, liquid measures, fork, plate, muffin pan, cooking spray, large bowl, mixing spoon, medium bowl, wooden toothpick, oven mitts, wire rack

1.			
All-purpose flour	2 cups	500 mL
Brown sugar, packed	3/4 cup	175 mL
Baking powder	1 tsp.	5 mL
Baking soda	1/2 tsp.	2 mL
Salt	1/2 tsp.	2 mL
2.		
Large egg	1	1
Mashed overripe banana **(about 3 medium)**	1 1/2 cups	375 mL
Milk	1/2 cup	125 mL
Butter, melted	1/3 cup	75 mL
Vanilla extract	1 tsp.	5 mL
3.		
Mini semi-sweet chocolate chips	1/2 cup	125 mL

1. Place oven rack in centre position. Turn oven on to 375°F (190°C). Grease muffin cups with cooking spray. Set aside. Put first 5 ingredients into large bowl. Stir. Dig a hole in centre of flour mixture with mixing spoon.

2. Break egg into medium bowl. Beat egg a little with fork. Add next 4 ingredients. Stir well. Pour into hole in flour mixture.

3. Add chocolate chips. Stir just until flour mixture is moistened. Fill muffin cups 3/4 full with batter. Bake for about 25 minutes until toothpick inserted straight down into centre of a muffin comes out clean. Put pan on wire rack. Turn oven off. Let cool for 5 minutes. Transfer muffins from pan to wire rack to cool. Makes 12 muffins.

1 muffin: 248 Calories; 8.4 g Total Fat (2.4 g Mono, 0.4 g Poly, 5.1 g Sat); 30 mg Cholesterol; 41 g Carbohydrate; 2 g Fibre; 4 g Protein; 224 mg Sodium

Pictured on page 105.

Monsieur Auk-Auk Tip: To melt butter, measure butter into small microwave-safe dish. Microwave on high (100%) for 10 seconds. Stir until melted.

Store the muffins in an airtight container or wrapped individually in plastic wrap in the freezer for up to 1 month.

No-Fluster Clusters

Hey Buster, don't fluster—these peanut butter and raisin clusters
are E-Z to make.

Get It Together: dry measures, measuring spoons, baking sheet with sides,
waxed paper, large bowl, medium bowl, mixing spoons

1.	Cornflakes cereal	2 cups	500 mL
	Chopped pecans	1/4 cup	60 mL
	Raisins	1/4 cup	60 mL
2.	Miniature marshmallows	2 cups	500 mL
	Smooth peanut butter	1/4 cup	60 mL
	Butter	2 tbsp.	30 mL

1. Line baking sheet with waxed paper. Set aside. Put first 3 ingredients
    into large bowl. Mix well.

2. Put remaining 3 ingredients into medium bowl. Microwave
    on high (100%) for 1 minute. Stir. Microwave for another 1 minute.
    Stir until smooth. Pour over cereal mixture. Stir until coated.
    Drop by tablespoonfuls onto baking sheet. Wait for about
    5 minutes until firm. Makes 18 clusters.

*1 cluster: 84 Calories; 4.3 g Total Fat (1.9 g Mono, 0.9 g Poly, 1.3 g Sat); 3 mg Cholesterol;
10 g Carbohydrate; 1 g Fibre; 1 g Protein; 38 mg Sodium*

Pictured on page 105.

Monsieur Auk-Auk Tip: Clusters can be individually
wrapped in plastic wrap or placed in an airtight container
and left at room temperature for up to 5 days. They can
also be stored in the freezer for up to 1 month.

1. Gold Rush Muffins, page 102
2. Fanana Of Banana Muffins, page 103
3. No-Fluster Clusters, above

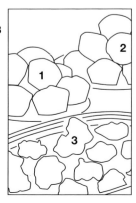

Plan It!

Left: Lemon Pineapple Ice Bombs, page 107 Right: Smoothie-On-A-Stick, below

Smoothie-On-A-Stick

It's a slick trick to lick a smoothie if it's on a stick!

Get It Together: liquid measures, sharp knife, cutting board, measuring spoons, blender, 8 paper cups (5 oz., 142 mL, size), muffin pan, foil, 8 wooden craft sticks

1.	Strawberry yogurt	1 1/2 cups	375 mL
	Sliced banana	1 cup	250 mL
	Milk	3/4 cup	175 mL
	Orange juice	3/4 cup	175 mL
	Vanilla extract	1/2 tsp.	2 mL

1. Put all 5 ingredients into blender. Cover with lid. Blend until smooth. Place 1 paper cup in each muffin cup. Pour yogurt mixture into paper cups until 3/4 full. Cover top of each cup with foil. Cut a small slit in centre of each piece of foil. Insert 1 stick through each slit almost to bottom of cup. Freeze overnight until firm. To loosen, run bottom of each cup under hot water for 3 to 4 seconds. While holding stick, push from bottom of cup to remove smoothie. Makes 8 smoothies.

1 smoothie: 87 Calories; 1.1 g Total Fat (trace Mono, trace Poly, 0.6 g Sat); 5 mg Cholesterol; 17 g Carbohydrate; trace Fibre; 3 g Protein; 37 mg Sodium

Pictured above.

Plan It!

Lemon Pineapple Ice Bombs

Get blown away by the explosion of lemon and pineapple flavour!

Get It Together: can opener, ice cream scoop, dry measures, medium bowl, mixing spoon, 10 paper cups (5 oz., 142 mL, size), muffin pan, foil, 10 wooden craft sticks

1.			
Can of lemon pie filling	19 oz.	540 mL
Butterscotch ripple ice cream, softened	2 cups	500 mL
Can of crushed pineapple, drained	14 oz.	398 mL

1. Put first 3 ingredients into bowl. Mix well. Place 1 paper cup in each muffin cup. Spoon about 1/2 cup (125 mL) ice cream mixture into each paper cup. Cover top of each cup with foil. Cut a small slit in centre of each piece of foil. Insert 1 stick through each slit almost to bottom of cup. Freeze overnight until firm. To loosen, run bottom of each cup under hot water for 3 to 4 seconds. While holding stick, push from bottom of cup to remove ice bomb. Makes 10 ice bombs.

1 ice bomb: 320 Calories; 10.8 g Total Fat (1.6 g Mono, 0.8 g Poly, 5.3 g Sat); 119 mg Cholesterol; 52 g Carbohydrate; 1 g Fibre; 5 g Protein; 72 mg Sodium

Pictured on page 106.

Monsieur Auk-Auk Tip: To soften ice cream, measure the amount you need and let it sit on the counter for about 5 minutes.

Q: Why did the cookie go to the doctor?

A: He was feeling crummy.

Cinnamon Hearts

These heart-shaped treats make a perfect gift when you want to say "I ♥ U."

Get It Together: measuring spoons, small bowl, mixing spoon, baking sheet with sides, cooking spray, oven mitts, wire rack

1.	Granulated sugar	2 tbsp.	30 mL
	Ground cinnamon	1 1/2 tsp.	7 mL
2.	Tube of plain bread stick dough	11 oz.	311 g

1. Place oven rack in centre position. Turn oven on to 350°F (175°C). Grease baking sheet with cooking spray. Set aside. Put sugar and cinnamon into bowl. Stir.

2. Unroll dough. Sprinkle dough with sugar mixture. Separate dough into 8 strips along perforations. Roll and twist strips to 14 inches (35 cm) long.

Form strips into a heart. Pinch dough at top and bottom points of heart.

Place hearts on baking sheet. Bake for 18 to 20 minutes until golden. Put baking sheet on wire rack. Turn oven off. Let cool for 5 minutes. Makes 8 hearts.

1 heart: 123 Calories; 2.0 g Total Fat (0 g Mono, 0 g Poly, 0 g Sat); 0 mg Cholesterol; 22 g Carbohydrate; 1 g Fibre; 3 g Protein; 290 mg Sodium

Pictured on page 109.

Monsieur Auk-Auk Tip: Store the hearts in an airtight container or wrapped individually in plastic wrap in the freezer for up to 1 month. To reheat, microwave the frozen heart on high (100%) for about 15 seconds until warm.

1. Hop Butterscotch Wedges, page 110
2. Cinnamon Hearts, above
3. Fairground Squares, page 111

108 **Plan It!**

Hop Butterscotch Wedges

Go triangular and replace your lunchtime granola bar with this deliciously sweet oat wedge!

Get It Together: dry measures, measuring spoons, sharp knife, cutting board, liquid measures, medium bowl, mixing spoon, small bowl, whisk, 9 inch (22 cm) microwave-safe pie plate, cooking spray

1.	Large flake rolled oats	2 cups	500 mL
	Butterscotch chips	1/2 cup	125 mL
	Brown sugar, packed	6 tbsp.	100 mL
	Chopped almonds	2 tbsp.	30 mL
	Salt	1/4 tsp.	1 mL
2.	Large egg	1	1
	Butter, melted	1/4 cup	60 mL
	Corn syrup	1/4 cup	60 mL
	Vanilla extract	1 tsp.	5 mL

1. Put first 5 ingredients into medium bowl. Stir.

2. Break egg into small bowl. Beat with whisk until egg is bubbly on top. Add remaining 3 ingredients. Mix well. Add to oat mixture. Mix well. Grease pie plate with cooking spray. Spread oat mixture evenly in pie plate. Microwave on high (100%) for 6 minutes. Let cool for 5 minutes. Cuts into 8 wedges.

1 wedge: 305 Calories; 12.2 g Total Fat (3.2 g Mono, 1.2 g Poly, 6.8 g Sat); 38 mg Cholesterol; 44 g Carbohydrate; 3 g Fibre; 5 g Protein; 151 mg Sodium

Pictured on page 109.

Monsieur Auk-Auk Tip: To melt butter, measure butter into small microwave-safe dish. Microwave on high (100%) for 10 seconds. Stir until melted.

If you don't have a microwave-safe pie plate, you can use a dinner plate instead.

Keep the wedges in an airtight container or wrap them individually in plastic wrap. Store them at room temperature for up to 3 days or in the freezer for up to 1 month.

Plan It!

Fairground Squares

Just like a caramel apple—but without the stick! Look for the caramel apple wraps in the produce section of your grocery store.

Get It Together: liquid measures, sharp knife, cutting board, dry measures, 9 x 9 inch (22 x 22 cm) pan, cooking spray, medium bowl, mixing spoon, large bowl, oven mitts, wire rack

1.	Diced peeled apple	3 cups	750 mL
	Lemon juice	1/4 cup	60 mL
2.	All-purpose flour	1 1/2 cups	375 mL
	Quick-cooking rolled oats	1 1/4 cups	300 mL
	Brown sugar, packed	1/2 cup	125 mL
	Butter	1 cup	250 mL
3.	Caramel apple wraps	5	5

1. Place oven rack in centre position. Turn oven on to 350°F (175°C). Grease pan with cooking spray. Set aside. Put apple and lemon juice into medium bowl. Stir until coated.

2. Put next 3 ingredients into large bowl. Stir. Rub in butter with your fingers until mixture resembles coarse crumbs. Press 2/3 of oat mixture into bottom of baking pan. Spread apple mixture over top.

3. Place caramel wraps over apple mixture, slightly overlapping. Sprinkle remaining oat mixture over top. Press down gently. Bake for about 30 minutes until golden. Put pan on wire rack. Turn oven off. Let cool for 5 minutes. Cuts into 16 squares.

1 square: 247 Calories; 13.1 g Total Fat (2.9 g Mono, 0.4 g Poly, 8.3 g Sat); 30 mg Cholesterol; 30 g Carbohydrate; 1 g Fibre; 3 g Protein; 117 mg Sodium

Pictured on page 109.

Monsieur Auk-Auk Tip: Store these squares in an airtight container or covered with plastic wrap in the refrigerator for up to 5 days. Or, store them in the freezer for up to 1 month.

Q: Why did the turkey cross the road twice?

A: To prove he wasn't a chicken.

Top: Love That Lemon Squares, page 113 Bottom: I Dream Of Square Cookies, below

I Dream Of Square Cookies

OK, these fluffy treats may not be square cookies, but they are cookie squares.

Get It Together: dry measures, medium bowl, fork, mixing spoon,
8 x 8 inch (20 x 20 cm) pan, foil, sharp knife

1.	Cream cheese, softened	4 oz.	125 g
	Icing (confectioner's) sugar	1/2 cup	125 mL
	Smooth peanut butter	1/2 cup	125 mL
2.	Frozen whipped topping, thawed	2 cups	500 mL
	Crushed chocolate chip cookies	1 cup	250 mL

1. Put cream cheese into bowl. Mash with fork until smooth. Add icing sugar and peanut butter. Stir until smooth.

2. Add whipped topping and cookies. Mix well. Line pan with foil. Spoon cookie mixture into pan. Spread evenly. Freeze for about 2 hours until firm. Cuts into 16 squares.

1 square: 149 Calories; 10.6 g Total Fat (2.0 g Mono, 1.1 g Poly, 5.1 g Sat); 10 mg Cholesterol; 13 g Carbohydrate; trace Fibre; 3 g Protein; 51 mg Sodium

Pictured above.

Monsieur Auk-Auk Tip: To soften cream cheese, let it sit on the counter for about 30 minutes.

Once frozen, cut and wrap squares individually in plastic wrap. Store them in the freezer for a convenient snack.

Love That Lemon Squares

These squares are a way-cool frozen treat with a chocolate crumb crust.

Get It Together: dry measures, liquid measures, small saucepan, mixing spoon, 9 x 9 inch (22 x 22 cm) pan, blender, sharp knife, cutting board

1.			
Butter		1/4 cup	60 mL
Chocolate wafer crumbs		1 1/4 cups	300 mL
Brown sugar, packed		1/4 cup	60 mL

2.			
Frozen whipped topping, thawed		4 cups	1 L
Milk		1 cup	250 mL
Box of instant lemon pudding powder (4-serving size)		1	1

3.			
Lemon jellied candy slices		8	8

1. Melt butter in saucepan. Add wafer crumbs and brown sugar. Stir well. Remove pan from heat. Press wafer crumb mixture into pan.

2. Put next 3 ingredients into blender. Cover with lid. Blend until smooth. Pour over wafer crumb mixture in pan. Spread evenly. Freeze for at least 4 hours until firm. Cut into 16 squares.

3. Cut candy slices in half. Gently press 1 half on each square. Makes 16 squares.

1 square: 163 Calories; 8.4 g Total Fat (1.2 g Mono, 0.5 g Poly, 6.4 g Sat); 9 mg Cholesterol; 22 g Carbohydrate; trace Fibre; 1 g Protein; 124 mg Sodium

Pictured on page 112.

> **Monsieur Auk-Auk Tip:** Instead of lemon pudding powder, use another flavour such as chocolate or butterscotch. To decorate, use chocolate chips or candy-coated chocolates.
>
> Store the frozen squares in an airtight container or individually wrapped in plastic wrap in the freezer for up to 1 month.

Q: What happens if you tell an egg a joke?

A: It cracks up.

Swirling Dervish Cookies

Round and round these dizzying treats go.

Get It Together: dry measures, measuring spoons, 2 small bowls, mixing spoon, large bowl, rolling pin, waxed paper, table knife, plastic wrap, cutting board, serrated knife, cookie sheets, cooking spray, oven mitts, wire racks

1.	Chocolate hazelnut spread	1/2 cup	125 mL
	Crushed walnuts	1/3 cup	75 mL
2.	All-purpose flour	1 1/4 cups	300 mL
	Baking powder	1/4 tsp.	1 mL
	Salt	1/4 tsp.	1 mL
3.	Butter, softened	1/2 cup	125 mL
	Granulated sugar	1/2 cup	125 mL
	Egg yolk (large)	1	1
	Vanilla extract	1/4 tsp.	1 mL

1. Put chocolate spread and walnuts into 1 small bowl. Mix well.

2. Put next 3 ingredients into other small bowl. Mix well.

3. Put butter and sugar into large bowl. Stir. Add egg yolk. Beat well. Add vanilla. Beat until smooth. Add half of flour mixture. Stir to combine. Add remaining flour mixture. Stir to combine. Shape dough into a ball. Place dough on sheet of waxed paper. Flatten dough into a rectangle. Place second sheet of waxed paper over top. Roll out dough to 8 x 10 inch (20 x 25 cm) rectangle. Discard top sheet of waxed paper. Spread chocolate mixture over dough, leaving a 1/2 inch (12 mm) border at each long edge. Roll up tightly from long side, jelly roll-style, using waxed paper as a guide. Press seam against roll to seal. Wrap with plastic wrap. Chill for about 1 hour until firm. Place oven rack in centre position. Turn oven on to 350°F (175°C). Grease cookie sheets with cooking spray. Set aside. Place roll, seam-side down, on cutting board. Cut with serrated knife into 1/4 inch (6 mm) slices. Arrange slices on cookie sheets, about 1 inch (2.5 cm) apart. Bake for 10 to 12 minutes until golden. Put cookie sheets on wire racks. Turn oven off. Let cool for 5 minutes. Transfer cookies to wire racks to cool. Makes about 36 cookies.

1 cookie: 78 Calories; 4.6 g Total Fat (1.5 g Mono, 0.9 g Poly, 1.9 g Sat); 12 mg Cholesterol; 8 g Carbohydrate; trace Fibre; 1 g Protein; 38 mg Sodium

Pictured on page 115.

(continued on next page)

Top: **Swirling Dervish Cookies**, above
Bottom: **Slammin' Jam Tarts**, page 116

Plan It!

Monsieur Auk-Auk Tip: To soften butter, let it sit on the counter for about 1 hour.

If you don't have an egg separator, you can separate the yolk from the egg white by cracking the egg as close to the middle as possible, being careful not to break the yolk. Hold the half of the shell with the yolk in it in one hand and the other half of the shell in the other hand. Allow as much of the egg white as possible to run out of the shell and into a small bowl. Then, transfer the yolk to the other half of the shell, allowing more of the egg white to run out. Repeat, a few times, until most of the egg white has been removed.

For fresh baked cookies anytime, after rolling the dough, wrap the roll in plastic wrap and freeze it. When you want fresh baked cookies, take the roll out of the freezer and wait for 10 minutes. Unwrap the roll and slice as many cookies as you like and bake them as directed.

Slammin' Jam Tarts

With lemon and berry, these tarts are completely jam-packed.

Get It Together: measuring spoons, dry measures, baking sheet with sides, oven mitts, wire rack, spoon

1.	Unbaked tart shells	8	8
2.	Spreadable cream cheese	8 tsp.	40 mL
3.	Lemon spread (or curd)	1/2 cup	125 mL
4.	Mixed berry jam	8 tsp.	40 mL

1. Place oven rack in centre position. Turn oven on to 375°F (190°C). Place tart shells on baking sheet. Bake for 10 to 12 minutes until golden. Put baking sheet on wire rack. Turn oven off. Let cool for 5 minutes.

2. Place 1 tsp. (5 mL) cream cheese in each tart. Gently spread cream cheese in bottom of tarts using spoon.

3. Spoon 1 tbsp. (15 mL) lemon spread over cream cheese. Spread evenly.

4. Spoon 1 tsp. (5 mL) jam in centre of each tart. Chill for about 1 hour until firm. Makes 8 tarts.

1 tart: 189 Calories; 9.0 g Total Fat (3.5 g Mono, 1.0 g Poly, 3.5 g Sat); 27 mg Cholesterol; 25 g Carbohydrate; trace Fibre; 2 g Protein; 153 mg Sodium

Pictured on page 115.

Monsieur Auk-Auk Tip: Store the tarts in an airtight container or covered with plastic wrap in the refrigerator for up to 2 days or in the freezer for up to 1 month.

Q: **What did the hungry computer eat?**

A: Microchips— 1 byte at a time.

Chocolate Dollar Dippers

These mini chocolate pancakes are great for dipping in yogurt, pudding or applesauce.

Get It Together: dry measures, liquid measures, measuring spoons, large bowl, mixing spoon, small bowl, whisk, large frying pan, pancake lifter, large plate, foil

1.	**Pancake mix**	1 1/4 cups	300 mL
2.	**Large egg**	1	1
	Chocolate milk	1 cup	250 mL
3.	**Cooking oil**	1 – 3 tsp.	5 – 15 mL

1. Put pancake mix into large bowl. Dig a hole in centre of pancake mix with mixing spoon.

2. Break egg into small bowl. Add milk. Beat with whisk until mixture is bubbly on top. Pour into hole in pancake mix. Stir just until pancake mix is moistened. The batter will be lumpy.

3. Heat 1 tsp. (5 mL) cooking oil in frying pan on medium-low for 3 minutes. Measure batter into pan, using about 1 tbsp. (15 mL) for each pancake. Cook for about 1 minute until bubbles form on top and edges of pancakes look dry. Use lifter to turn pancakes over. Cook for another 1 minute until bottoms are golden. Use lifter to check. Remove pancakes to plate. Cover with foil to keep warm. Repeat with remaining batter, heating more cooking oil in pan before each batch, if necessary, so pancakes won't stick. Makes about 32 dippers.

1 pancake: 25 Calories; 0.5 g Total Fat (0.2 g Mono, 0.1 g Poly, 0.2 g Sat); 6 mg Cholesterol; 4 g Carbohydrate; trace Fibre; 1 g Protein; 64 mg Sodium

Pictured on page 119.

Monsieur Auk-Auk Tip: Store the cooled pancakes in an airtight container in the fridge for up to 3 days, or in the freezer for up to 1 month. To eat cold, thaw frozen pancakes at room temperature for about 20 minutes. To reheat, place 5 to 10 pancakes on a plate. Microwave on high (100%) for 20 to 30 seconds until warm.

Granola Grab Bags

Grab these ready-to-eat bags of granola whenever you're on the go.
Eat it right out of the bag or sprinkle it on yogurt or ice cream.

Get It Together: dry measures, sharp knife, cutting board, measuring spoons, large saucepan, mixing spoons, baking sheet with sides, cooking spray, oven mitts, wire rack, large bowl, 6 resealable sandwich bags

1.	Brown sugar, packed	1/3 cup	75 mL
	Butter	1/4 cup	60 mL
2.	Quick-cooking rolled oats	2 1/2 cups	625 mL
	Chopped walnuts	1/4 cup	60 mL
	Slivered almonds	1/4 cup	60 mL
	Vanilla extract	1/2 tsp.	2 mL
	Ground cinnamon	1/8 tsp.	0.5 mL
3.	Dried cranberries	1/2 cup	125 mL
	Raisins	1/2 cup	125 mL
	Chopped dried apricot	1/4 cup	60 mL
	Semi-sweet chocolate chips	1/4 cup	60 mL

1. Place oven rack in centre position. Turn oven on to 350°F (175°C). Grease baking sheet with cooking spray. Set aside. Put brown sugar and butter into saucepan. Heat and stir on medium until melted and smooth. Remove pan from heat.

2. Add next 5 ingredients. Stir until coated. Spoon oat mixture onto baking sheet. Spread evenly. Bake for 10 to 15 minutes, stirring occasionally, until golden. Put baking sheet on wire rack. Turn oven off. Wait for about 30 minutes until cool. Transfer to bowl.

3. Add remaining 4 ingredients. Use mixing spoons to toss until combined. Spoon about 3/4 cup (175 mL) into each sandwich bag. Makes 6 grab bags.

1 grab bag: 439 Calories; 18.5 g Total Fat (5.0 g Mono, 3.4 g Poly, 6.6 g Sat); 20 mg Cholesterol; 65 g Carbohydrate; 7 g Fibre; 8 g Protein; 67 mg Sodium

Pictured on page 119.

Monsieur Auk-Auk Tip:
The grab bags can be stored at room temperature for up to 5 days.

Top: Granola Grab Bags, above

Bottom: Chocolate Dollar Dippers, page 117

Hokey Pokey Squares

You put some of this in. You take nothing out.
You put some of that in—and you stir it all about!

Get It Together: dry measures, measuring spoons, large bowl, small saucepan, mixing spoon, 9 x 9 inch (22 x 22 cm) pan, cooking spray, sharp knife

1.			
Broken stick pretzels	1 1/4 cups	300 mL
Crisp rice cereal	1 cup	250 mL
Candy-coated chocolates	3/4 cup	175 mL
Dry-roasted peanuts	1/4 cup	60 mL

2.			
Miniature marshmallows	2 1/2 cups	625 mL
Butter	1/4 cup	60 mL
Smooth peanut butter	2 tbsp.	30 mL

1. Put first 4 ingredients into bowl. Mix well.

2. Put remaining 3 ingredients into saucepan. Heat and stir on medium until melted. Pour marshmallow mixture over pretzel mixture. Stir until pretzel mixture is coated. Grease pan with cooking spray. Spoon mixture into pan. Spread evenly and press down with back of spoon. Let cool for about 10 minutes until firm. Cuts into 16 squares.

1 square: 263 Calories; 12.4 g Total Fat (4.2 g Mono, 1.0 g Poly, 6.7 g Sat); 12 mg Cholesterol; 35 g Carbohydrate; 1 g Fibre; 3 g Protein; 163 mg Sodium

Pictured on front cover.

Monsieur Auk-Auk Tip: For easier packing, after spreading the mixture in the pan, lay a sheet of waxed paper over top and press down evenly with your hands.

Store these squares in an airtight container at room temperature for up to 3 days.

Q: Why did the cow cross the road?

A: It was the chicken's day off.

Measurement Tables

Throughout this book measurements are given in Conventional and Metric measure. To compensate for differences between the two measurements due to rounding, a full metric measure is not always used. The cup used is the standard 8 fluid ounce. Temperature is given in degrees Fahrenheit and Celsius. Baking pan measurements are in inches and centimetres as well as quarts and litres. An exact metric conversion is given below as well as the working equivalent (Metric Standard Measure).

Spoons

Conventional Measure	Metric Exact Conversion Millilitre (mL)	Metric Standard Measure Millilitre (mL)
1/8 teaspoon (tsp.)	0.6 mL	0.5 mL
1/4 teaspoon (tsp.)	1.2 mL	1 mL
1/2 teaspoon (tsp.)	2.4 mL	2 mL
1 teaspoon (tsp.)	4.7 mL	5 mL
2 teaspoons (tsp.)	9.4 mL	10 mL
1 tablespoon (tbsp.)	14.2 mL	15 mL

Cups

Conventional Measure	Metric Exact Conversion Millilitre (mL)	Metric Standard Measure Millilitre (mL)
1/4 cup (4 tbsp.)	56.8 mL	60 mL
1/3 cup (5 1/3 tbsp.)	75.6 mL	75 mL
1/2 cup (8 tbsp.)	113.7 mL	125 mL
2/3 cup (10 2/3 tbsp.)	151.2 mL	150 mL
3/4 cup (12 tbsp.)	170.5 mL	175 mL
1 cup (16 tbsp.)	227.3 mL	250 mL
4 1/2 cups	1022.9 mL	1000 mL (1 L)

Oven Temperatures

Fahrenheit (°F)	Celsius (°C)
175°	80°
200°	95°
225°	110°
250°	120°
275°	140°
300°	150°
325°	160°
350°	175°
375°	190°
400°	205°
425°	220°
450°	230°
475°	240°
500°	260°

Dry Measurements

Conventional Measure Ounces (oz.)	Metric Exact Conversion Grams (g)	Metric Standard Measure Grams (g)
1 oz.	28.3 g	28 g
2 oz.	56.7 g	57 g
3 oz.	85.0 g	85 g
4 oz.	113.4 g	125 g
5 oz.	141.7 g	140 g
6 oz.	170.1 g	170 g
7 oz.	198.4 g	200 g
8 oz.	226.8 g	250 g
16 oz.	453.6 g	500 g
32 oz.	907.2 g	1000 g (1 kg)

Pans

Conventional Inches	Metric Centimetres
8x8 inch	20x20 cm
9x9 inch	22x22 cm
9x13 inch	22x33 cm
10x15 inch	25x38 cm
11x17 inch	28x43 cm
8x2 inch round	20x5 cm
9x2 inch round	22x5 cm
10x4 1/2 inch tube	25x11 cm
8x4x3 inch loaf	20x10x7.5 cm
9x5x3 inch loaf	22x12.5x7.5 cm

Casseroles

CANADA & BRITAIN		UNITED STATES	
Standard Size Casserole	Exact Metric Measure	Standard Size Casserole	Exact Metric Measure
1 qt. (5 cups)	1.13 L	1 qt. (4 cups)	900 mL
1 1/2 qts. (7 1/2 cups)	1.69 L	1 1/2 qts. (6 cups)	1.35 L
2 qts. (10 cups)	2.25 L	2 qts. (8 cups)	1.8 L
2 1/2 qts. (12 1/2 cups)	2.81 L	2 1/2 qts. (10 cups)	2.25 L
3 qts. (15 cups)	3.38 L	3 qts. (12 cups)	2.7 L
4 qts. (20 cups)	4.5 L	4 qts. (16 cups)	3.6 L
5 qts. (25 cups)	5.63 L	5 qts. (20 cups)	4.5 L

Recipe Index

A

B

C

D

E

F

G

Recipe Index   123

H

I

J

K

L

Recipe Index

Recipe Index   125

Company's Coming cookbooks are available at retail locations throughout Canada!

EXCLUSIVE mail order offer on next page

Buy any 2 cookbooks—choose a 3rd FREE of equal or lesser value than the lowest price paid.

Original Series — CA$15.99 Canada — US$12.99 USA & International

CODE		CODE		CODE	
SQ	150 Delicious Squares	CFK	Cook For Kids	WM	30-Minute Weekday Meals
CA	Casseroles	SCH	Stews, Chilies & Chowders	SDL	School Days Lunches
MU	Muffins & More	FD	Fondues	PD	Potluck Dishes
SA	Salads	CCBE	The Beef Book	GBR	Ground Beef Recipes
AP	Appetizers	RC	The Rookie Cook	FRIR	4-Ingredient Recipes
SS	Soups & Sandwiches	RHR	Rush-Hour Recipes	KHC	Kids' Healthy Cooking
CO	Cookies	SW	Sweet Cravings	MM	Mostly Muffins
PA	Pasta	YRG	Year-Round Grilling	SP	Soups
BA	Barbecues	GG	Garden Greens	SU	Simple Suppers
PR	Preserves	CHC	Chinese Cooking	CCDC	Diabetic Cooking
CH	Chicken, Etc.	PK	The Pork Book	CHN	Chicken Now
CT	Cooking For Two	RL	Recipes For Leftovers	KDS	Kids Do Snacks
SC	Slow Cooker Recipes	EB	The Egg Book	TMRC	30-Minute Rookie Cook
SF	Stir-Fry	SDPP	School Days Party Pack		**NEW** *September 1/07*
MAM	Make-Ahead Meals	HS	Herbs & Spices		
PB	The Potato Book	BEV	The Beverage Book		
CCLFC	Low-Fat Cooking	SCD	Slow Cooker Dinners		

Cookbook Author Biography

CODE	CA$15.99 Canada US$12.99 USA & International
JP	Jean Paré: An Appetite for Life

Most Loved Recipe Collection

CODE	CA$23.99 Canada US$19.99 USA & International
MLA	Most Loved Appetizers
MLMC	Most Loved Main Courses
MLT	Most Loved Treats
MLBQ	Most Loved Barbecuing
MLCO	Most Loved Cookies

CODE	CA$24.99 Canada US$19.99 USA & International
MLSD	Most Loved Salads & Dressings
MLCA	Most Loved Casseroles
MLSF	Most Loved Stir-Fries

3-in-1 Cookbook Collection

CODE	CA$29.99 Canada US$24.99 USA & International
QEE	Quick & Easy Entertaining
MNT	Meals in No Time

Lifestyle Series

CODE	CA$17.99 Canada US$15.99 USA & International
DC	Diabetic Cooking

CODE	CA$19.99 Canada US$15.99 USA & International
DDI	Diabetic Dinners
LCR	Low-Carb Recipes
HR	Easy Healthy Recipes
HH	Healthy in a Hurry
WGR	Whole Grain Recipes
	NEW *August 1/07*

Special Occasion Series

CODE	CA$20.99 Canada US$19.99 USA & International
GFK	Gifts from the Kitchen

CODE	CA$24.99 Canada US$19.99 USA & International
BSS	Baking—Simple to Sensational
CGFK	Christmas Gifts from the Kitchen
TR	Timeless Recipes for All Occasions

CODE	CA$27.99 Canada US$22.99 USA & International
CCEL	Christmas Celebrations

Order ONLINE for fast delivery!

Log onto **www.companyscoming.com**, browse through our library of cookbooks, gift sets and newest releases and place your order using our fast and secure online order form.

Buy 2, Get 1 FREE!

Buy any 2 cookbooks—choose a **3rd FREE** of equal or lesser value than the lowest price paid.

Title	Code	Quantity	Price	Total
			$	$
DON'T FORGET to indicate your FREE BOOK(S). (see exclusive mail order offer above) please print				

| | | TOTAL BOOKS (including FREE) | | TOTAL BOOKS PURCHASED: | $ |

	International	USA	Canada
Shipping & Handling First Book (per destination)	$ 11.98 (one book)	$ 6.98 (one book)	$ 5.98 (one book)
Additional Books (include FREE books)	$ ($4.99 each)	$ ($1.99 each)	$ ($1.99 each)
Sub-Total	$	$	$
Canadian residents add GST/HST			$
TOTAL AMOUNT ENCLOSED	$	$	$

Terms

- All orders must be prepaid. Sorry, no CODs.
- Prices are listed in Canadian Funds for Canadian orders, or US funds for US & International orders.
- Prices are subject to change without prior notice.
- Canadian residents must pay GST/HST (no provincial tax required).
- No tax is required for orders outside Canada.
- Satisfaction is guaranteed or return within 30 days for a full refund.
- Make cheque or money order payable to: **Company's Coming Publishing Limited** 2311-96 Street, Edmonton, Alberta Canada T6N 1G3.
- Orders are shipped surface mail. For courier rates, visit our website: **www.companyscoming.com** or contact us: **Tel: 780-450-6223 Fax: 780-450-1857.**

Gift Giving

- Let us help you with your gift giving!
- We will send cookbooks directly to the recipients of your choice if you give us their names and addresses.
- Please specify the titles you wish to send to each person.
- If you would like to include a personal note or card, we will be pleased to enclose it with your gift order.
- Company's Coming Cookbooks make excellent gifts: birthdays, bridal showers, Mother's Day, Father's Day, graduation or any occasion ...collect them all!

☐ MasterCard   ☐ VISA   Expiry _____ / _____   MO/YR

Credit Card # _____

Name of cardholder _____

Cardholder signature _____

Shipping Address Send the cookbooks listed above to:

☐ **Please check if this is a Gift Order**

Name: _____

Street: _____

City: _____ Prov./State: _____

Postal Code/Zip: _____ Country: _____

Tel: (_____) _____

E-mail address: _____

Your privacy is important to us. We will not share your e-mail address or personal information with any outside party.

☐ **YES! Please add me to your News Bite e-mail newsletter.**